Woman,

You Are Not Infertile

Veronica Anusionwu

The Lord's Word On Healing Series

The Lord's Word On Healing Publications

Books which I found useful for reference, are *Trying for a Baby* by Peter Moore (Lion Publishing) and the *BMA Family Health Encyclopedia* (Dorling Kindersley).

Unless otherwise indicated, bible quotes are from the *New International Version*, © 1973, 1978, 1984 by the International Bible Society, and used by kind permission of Hodder & Stoughton. Other editions quoted from include *The Amplified Bible, Old Testament,* © 1965, 1987 by the Zondervan Corporation; *The Amplified New Testament* © 1958, 1987 by the Lockman Foundation, used with kind permission, and *The King James Version of The Bible.*

ISBN 0-9532698-0-9

Scriptures in this book have been personalize to encourage individual application.

Printed and bound by Professional Book Supplies, Oxford, England

CONTENTS

Author's preface

Introduction

Page

iii

AUTHOR'S PREFACE

The Word of God is supernatural; mixing faith with the Word of God by speaking His words through your own mouth is a way of applying God's medicine. However, the Word of God only works by faith (simple belief that God meant what he said). If you do not have enough faith, go to your doctor to receive help, for God also uses doctors to perform miracles in people's lives and many lives are saved by doctors. The Word of God and the wisdom of your doctor will work togather to bless your life.

Our Lord Jesus Christ, after healing a man, sent him to go and have himself examined by his priest. (Priests were the doctors in those days; it was their duty to confirm the healing of the individual.) Luke 5: 14.

Do not throw your medicine away and rely on God's Word alone unless God tells you to do so.

Everything works by faith. See your doctor before you throw away your medication. Where there is no cure for your sickness then applying the Word of God by faith will surely bring about healing. When your faith grows you will be able to take God's Word for what your faith tells you, for God's Word can never fail. Use common sense and may God answer you in the day of trouble. (Psalms 20: 1)

NOTE

There are times you will read the word "man" in this book. Man here is not referring to gender as in male. But God call us all sons - both men and women. So, when you read, a righteous man, it is not referring to the "male" but to both sexes.

A note to doctors

I know the time will come when this book will come into the hands of those in the medical profession. God wants you to know that all medical problems are in his power. Where science has no answers you can use God's Word to make a difference. Every honest doctor will agree with me that the area of infertility has defied scientific research; this is because God has kept the final answer to Himself for his glory. Study this book carefully and question what is written and I pray that the Holy Spirit of God will help you to understand.

The will of man

God created each and every one of us with a will to choose. He gave us a will. God will never force anything on you or me, or ask us to do anything against our will. In his Word he has laid down the benefits of both good and evil but he advises us to choose good and do it. Our God will never do anything for anyone against their will. See the statements made by the Lord Jesus Christ like "if any man wills, let him come unto me and drink, if any man will open the door, I will come unto him and sup with him and him with me."

Man's consent is the first step into divine blessing. Christ is willing to help the helpless anywhere if the helpless are willing to acknowledge their helplessness and reveal a readiness to be guided. So today, I want you to know that to receive God's blessing, you must be willing and you must ask for it.

Deliberate repetitions

There are quite a few repetitions in this book, especially God's promises; why have I done this? Because whatever you read or hear again and again sticks in your memory. Why do you think CNN repeat the same news again and again. Because they want people to remember that news. So the repetitions are deliberate so that you will always remember God's promises to you.

God's method

> "For my thoughts are not your thoughts, neither are my
> ways your ways," declares the Lord. "As the Heavens are
> higher than the earth, so are my ways higher than your
> ways and my thoughts than your thoughts." Isaiah 55:8-9

Throughout this book, you will not read material anywhere about methods, because God does not work with methods. God will always manifest himself in your life because He always confirm his words, but the methods he has decided to use are always left to him. He will not allow us to reduce him to a recipe. Time and time again, I have seen God confirm His Word in the life of his people. The problem may be the same but the way He manifests Himself is always different in every case.

He will never show himself the same way twice. The Bible says, "His mercies are new every morning for great is his faithfulness." I have prayed for so many people, perhaps on the road as I go shopping or on an outing, and also many times in my own personal life, but he has never manifested Himself the same way twice. I have seen instant manifestation in prayers while other times there has been a waiting period before a visible manifestation is noticed. In all cases God hears the first prayers and answers them immediately but the final result and timing is best left to Him - the all-knowing and all-sufficient God. If you are trusting God's words, and His promise, hold fast; it may tarry, but it will surely come.

Women's confessions

These confessions which have placed in the relevant place throughout the book are general confessions which you should be able to confess every day until there is full manifestation of your desires. I have Kept them short, so that you can memorise them and keep confessing them until they grow and bear fruit in Jesus' name. Confess them as many times as you can, day and night. There are no side effects and it works. Remember to sit in a comfortable position and mediate on the promises of God you are confessing. God bless you.

INTRODUCTION

In the name that is above every name, the name of my Lord and Saviour, Jesus Christ, I welcome you to this book, part of *"The overcoming Infertility collection."* I am happy to present *The Lord's Word* to you. I am also happy to you tell you that Jesus loves you and wants you to know he is coming back again soon to take you home with him. Before He comes, He wants you to live a victorious life here on earth.

What a pleasure it has been for me just watching the great acts of our Lord and Saviour Jesus Christ come to life. Using things like bread and fish, saliva and mud, and water, we see the Bible miracles came alive once again to heal and restore us thousands of years after they were recorded. What about the story of David and Goliath written at least three to four thousand years ago? Yet it has never lost its power. Once again it appears here to bring healing and hope to those who think their victory is based on numbers rather than on God.

I am thrilled to be the vessel through which the Holy Spirit has brought about these books. The problem of infertility in our generation is not a small one. Over a hundred million couples are estimated to face this problem world-wide. Yet in the very heart of God is an overwhelming desire to bless all human beings with children. Today, I desire that we look away from the inadequacies of our medical researches to the banquet of rich food prepared for us by almighty God. Jesse Duplantis said about his trip to Heaven in his book (*Close Encounters Of The God Kind*):

> "I saw new lives of little babies singing and flying around God's throne. It seemed to be that babies just came out of the breath of God. They looked like they were wearing night gowns.
> They flew into the presence of Jehovah. I realised they were new souls who came from the thoughts of God. God thinks kids. Now I know why those new-born babies are

so precious. Babies are gifts given to us directly from the throne of God."

I personally believe this is true, for God has given me a tiny glimpse into His love and desire for mankind - a desire to bless us with all that we ever desire or need.

Today, I invite you to come and partake of this great banquet prepared by almighty God. This book you are holding is a prayer; this book has been born in the ovens of prayer. I have prayed, I have cried and studied hard to be able to write this book. I have received so many miracles already that if you will fix your faith, babies are going to just come - Bam! Bam! Bam! It will amaze you. If you will dare to fix your faith (trust) in Jesus and His promise that is written for you, you will receive all your heart's desire so that your joy may be complete.

Never in my life have I known such love as the love that flows from the heart of God to all mankind. Reach out in trust like a little baby and receive it.

I have written these books to bring you joy and happiness in your home because that's what Jesus has commanded me to do. In this book I have written everything that you need to know about infertility, from the Bible, from the very heart of God. God has promised to bless you with all that you need so that your joy will be complete. I have written all the Lord has told me to write to His beloved men and women and I stand upon these promises because Jesus Christ is no mere man. No mere human could promise to solve all the problems of the world. But in His promise that he is able to meet all our needs, he proves once and for all that He alone is the great creator of the Heavens and the earth and all that is in it.

Today I encourage you to receive the truth written down and in doing so you will be mightily blessed. God Bless You And Remember Jesus Loves You.

Chapter One

The Role of The Holy Spirit In Your Life

In the Name that is above every name, the Name of our Lord and Saviour Jesus Christ, I welcome you to this book, and I would like to tell you this, *"**Jesus loves you and cares about you.**"*

My question to you today is this, "Do you know the Holy Spirit?" Consider if your answer to this question is no, then allow me to introduce you to Him, if your answer is yes I encourage you to read this chapter and get to know Him even more. He is the One Who wrote this book, to the *"**glory of Jesus Christ**,"* so that the blessings and goodness of God will come to you.

He is the One Whom Jesus left on earth for us. For the Lord Jesus Christ, before He left to go back to the Father, promised us this:

> I will ask the Father, and he will give you another
> Counsellor to be with you for ever - the Spirit of truth.
> The world cannot accept him, because it neither sees him
> nor knows him. But you know him, for he lives with you
> and will be in you. I will not leave you as orphans. I will
> come to you." (John 14: 16-18)

From this passage you can see that the Holy Spirit is already here on earth with us. isn't it possible to have Him with us and yet totally miss His presence and His love, because we have not taken the time to find out Who He is.

You say I call Him *"**He**"*. Yes, the Holy Spirit of God is a person. He is not a mere influence or force coming from God. He is a real

1

person. Jesus said, *"...that he may abide with you."* He is not an it. He is a real person. He is not just a power. He is a person.

The Holy Spirit speaks (Revelation 2: 11). A force cannot speak to people. The Holy Spirit comforts people-In John 14:16-18- He is described as the comforter. In Ephesians 4: 30 we see that the Holy Spirit can be grieved. A force cannot be grieved.

From these few Bible verses, you can see that the Holy Spirit is a person: In Romans 15: 30 -The Apostle Paul refers to the love of the Holy Spirit as the love of Christ.

> Before I continue, I beseech you brethren for the love of Christ, and the love of the Holy Spirit.

Have you ever thought of the love of the Holy Spirit? The love of God the Father is the love of the Holy Spirit - "The love of the Spirit is the love of Jesus Christ, which caused Him to leave His throne in Heaven and come down to earth to dwell in the midst of selfish, sinful men. It is the love that led Him to bleed to death on the Cross; having loved His own, He loved them to the end. For God so loved the world that He gave His only Son. (John 3: 16).

That is the unconditional love of God, without which the whole world would have been lost. It is the love of the Son, which no human language is able to express. It is deeper than the deepest sea. Yet today, I will say this to you, the love of the Father would have been in vain; the self-sacrificing love of Jesus Christ of no purpose, if it had not been for that great, patient, infinite love of the blessed Holy Spirit working in our heart. The working of the Trinity is the mystery of the Gospel of Jesus Christ. It is better to accept it than to try to figure it out, for only in Heaven will we clearly understand it all. Take what you have and apply it and let it work for you.

My personal relationship with the Holy Spirit

I would like to share my testimony with you about the Holy Spirit, and the reason why I choose to start the first chapter of this book with the Holy Spirit.

I met the Holy Spirit for the first time in August 1992, the day I gave my heart to the Lord. After that service, I went to the bookshop of that church and I bought three books that laid a total foundation for my Christian walk. One of those books was *Good Morning Holy Spirit* by Benny Hinn. In it he shared with us about his relationship with the Holy Spirit and how he found out the Holy Spirit was a person, and what he did to establish his relationship with Him.

Being a new Christian and having no spiritual experience, I did what Benny had done. The next morning, I selected a corner in my daughter's room, put a rug there, sat down and I said, *"Good Morning Holy Spirit."* Immediately I said it, I felt His power and presence on me, and I started weeping. It was the most wonderful experience of my life. I then knew for myself that the Holy Spirit was a real person. I also learnt that the Holy Spirit was my Teacher, that if my Christian walk was going to be fruitful and successful, I was to know the Holy Spirit as a person.

Well, not only did I get to know Him as a person, I fell in love with Him. He started to teach me things from the Bible, and show me all that Jesus had done for me, and how the blood of Jesus had paid for all my sins, and provided for all I will ever need in life.

Within three weeks of knowing the Holy Spirit, something happened inside of me. I could no longer stand to see suffering or anyone sick. I started to pray for sick people on the road or in the bus, and God just healed them there on the spot. Seeing these miracles my faith in God grew and so did my desire to reach out for those in need. The Holy Spirit would wake me up at night to go and pray for someone, and He would heal them.

Within a period of six months of knowing the Holy Spirit, He had taught me so much. I can say to the glory of God that, because of my relationship with the Holy Spirit, I did not require any counselling or have any need to run up and down looking for people to answer my questions, because whatever problems I faced, He always dealt with them and answered all my questions, and directed me in all my ways. Everything I did, I consulted the Holy Spirit and He directed me.

Remember the Bible says, "In all your ways acknowledge the Lord, and He will direct your path." (Proverbs 3: 6) This is exactly my principle for walking with the Lord. I can boldly tell you that God has been faithful and true to His Word. The Holy Spirit has been my Comforter and my God. Throughout the years I have walked with the Lord, He has been true to His promise, he has guided me in all my ways and directed my footsteps. I can boldly declare to you that God is true and His Word perfect.

I have taken time to share just a little bit of my experience, to encourage you to get to know Him for yourself. This book is His work.

Every thing written in this book are only as a result of His help.

He gives faith

He gives faith as a gift (I Corinthians 12: 9). We may not know how He creates faith, but I think it is enough to know that He does.

Faith is one of His gifts even as faithfulness is part of His fruit. An example from the Bible is that of Stephen and Barnabas. They were men full of faith and the Holy Spirit (Acts 6: 5, Acts 11: 24); from this we can see that a special manifestation of faith is a result of fullness of the Holy Spirit.

The Holy Spirit creates the faith in our heart, through which we receive salvation. One of the ways He imparts faith in our hearts is through those that belong to Christ like Apostles, Prophets, Evangelists, Pastors and Teachers, etc. The Holy Spirit convicts the person of their sin as the word of God is proclaimed and creates in their heart the need for the Saviour.

To write this book has taken great faith on my part. And I tell you the truth, I would never have attempted it, if not for the fullness of God's Holy Spirit, and His faithfulness to me, and because of my love for my Lord Jesus, and my commitment to obey and serve Him. These are some of the benefits of knowing the Holy Spirit.

Physical life

The Holy Spirit is the One Who gives life, both spiritual and physical life. Before God could create anything on earth, the Holy Spirit was already there to breath life into whatever God said.

> Now the earth was formless and empty. Darkness was over the surface of the deep, and the Spirit of God was hovering over the waters. And God said, Let there be light, and there was light. (Genesis 1: 1-3)

The Bible says in the Psalms that when God sends His Spirit, that is when we are created.

The Holy Spirit is the One Who creates life. The Spirit gives life (John 6: 63). Every life on earth today is given by the Holy Spirit. Those of you who desire to have children, it is the Holy Spirit Who will give that life to the child in your womb. We hear the angel of God telling Mary:

> The Holy Spirit will come upon you, and the power of the Most High will overshadow you. (Luke 1: 35)

4

So it is the Spirit that gives life to a baby in the womb. Even when we become pregnant, no one can claim knowledge of the exact time conception took place. All these things are secret things that belong to God, but the important thing I want you to know is this, the Holy Spirit is the giver of life.

The Holy Spirit gives life to our mortal bodies (Romans 8: 11), which means that any death that exists in your body, can be resurrected by the Holy Spirit living inside you.

Spiritual life

It is the Holy Spirit who gives spiritual life. He is the One Who bestows it. He tends and nurtures that life. No man can redeem himself or sanctify himself. All these are works of the Holy Spirit. He works in us, creating in our heart the desire for a Saviour, leading us patiently to Jesus, and sustaining us.

A man can achieve only so much in his own strength, he can acquire knowledge by diligent study, but he cannot win for himself the life which is from God. Eternal life.

The modern man will say today, *"Seek your own salvation. All ways lead to God. We believe in freedom of religion."* Some will not direct their children in the way of God. "Oh, when he grows up, he will choose which God he wants to serve, because these days there are too many gods." But this new gospel of the modern man only leads to disappointment. If man could save himself, God would not have sacrificed His only Son for our redemption.

Salvation is a gift from God. The Holy Spirit alone can do what no human can do for us. He is the giver of life. "Not by works of righteousness which we have done, but according to His mercy He saved us by the washing of regeneration and renewing of the Holy Ghost. (Titus 3: 5)

Helping our weakness

The Bible says in Romans 8: 26 that the Holy Spirit helps our weaknesses. In our prayer we often find that we do not know what to pray. Many of you reading this book might never even have prayed before, but the Holy Spirit will teach you how to pray, according to the will of God. He will show you what you need and what to do in every situation you face. He creates in our heart a longing after more prayer. He glorifies

Christ. He shows us His glory. If you don't know how and what to pray, ask the Holy Spirit to help you pray. He will pray through you. You will have answers to prayers that will amaze you. You will experience that "He is able to do immeasurably more than all we can ask or imagine, according to the power that is at work within us." (Ephesians 3: 20)

The Holy Spirit sheds the love of God in our hearts (Romans 5: 5)

A lawyer may be very able in his profession without necessarily loving his clients. A doctor can have success without loving his patients. A businessman may prosper without loving his customers. But you can never be a worker of Christ without a deep passion for lost souls. Love alone is the key to the hearts of all men. Even the hardest heart cannot, in the long run, resist the influence of love. Why did our Lord leave His home in Heaven to come to this sinful earth? Was it not His great compassion and love which led Him to die on the Cross of Calvary?

> Greater love hath no man than this, that he lay down his life for his friend. (John 15: 13)

One day Paul was asked what drove him from land to land, from city to city. "After they stoned you at Lystra, why do you preach the same Gospel in Derbe? Why are you exposing yourself to many dangers?" His answer was simple and plain: *"The love of Christ compels us."* (2 Corinthians 5: 14)

When the Lord showed me my vision and the work he called me to do, these were His words to me: *"Veronica, to do this work, you will have to love everybody."* My first question to Him was, *"Lord, how is that possible?"* He told me it could be done by the Holy Spirit. Today, six years down the road, I can say to the glory of God that I am learning, day by day, to love everybody. When I look at people, all I see is Jesus Christ, the One Who created them in His image. I try to look away from their weaknesses, because I have a bag full of mine as well, but I look at them through the eyes of God, the eyes and heart full of love for all mankind.

Many of you reading this book may not know how to love God, because no one ever told you, but I can guarantee you, if you ask the Holy Spirit, he will shed the love of Christ abroad in your heart.

The Holy Spirit gives freedom

The Bible says, "Where the Spirit of the Lord is there is liberty." (II Corinthians 3: 17) There are many people today, even among the Christians, who are still bound by one thing or another, because they do not have the Spirit of Christ in them.

One day in a Sunday School Class, a teacher asked a boy if he could break a piece of thread. The boy smiled, "Of course I can do that." The teacher placed the boy in the middle of the class and had him bound with that thread until he could not move. The thread was stronger than the boy.

> But every man is tempted when he is drawn away of his own lust and enticed, then when lust hath conceived, it bringeth forth sin and sin, when it is finished, bringeth forth death. (James 1: 14)

The beginning of sin lies in our thoughts. We all have sinful imaginations, then a moment comes when we do not resist any more. The sinful thoughts become sinful acts, and when often repeated, become a sinful habit. Then the soul is bound. We may have life, but lack the freedom.

Take an example, the lion caged up in a zoo has life, but has no freedom. He wrestles in vain to be free. He beats the iron bars in vain. He can never free himself. Someone else must give him freedom.

Are you bound today? - by sickness, demonic oppression, etc? Then this is Who you need - the Holy Spirit of God, because, where the Spirit of God is, there is liberty. Be filled with the Spirit of God and all chains will fall. Do you want to be free, free from pain and sin? Do you really long for freedom? Then come to Jesus. He can help you.

How can I receive the Holy Spirit?

The world cannot receive the Holy Spirit, because they do not know Him. (*John 14: 17*). He comes to the children of God. The fullness and power of the Holy Spirit is for all God's children.

Those who, after reading this book, decide to invite the Lord into their heart to be their Saviour, will also receive the Holy Spirit. The fact that you have gone to church since you were born, does not help at all. You must personally invite Jesus to come into your heart and be your Lord and Saviour, then the Holy Spirit comes too. When He comes He helps you to grow spiritually, teaches you Who Jesus is, what your rights as a child of God are, and gives you all the benefits mentioned in

7

the Word of God.

Have you received the Holy Spirit?

In concluding this chapter on the Holy Spirit, I would like to share a sad story with you, which had a happy ending and I leave you today with this question. *What will you do with the Holy Spirit?*

The story of Mary

This is the story of Mary who was a widow. After a short, happy married life, her husband died, leaving her with their only son, Andrew. She was a poor widow, but all she wished was for her Andrew to have a good education. She worked day and night. No sacrifice was too much to make for her Andrew, and the son rewarded her by his hard work.

Eventually Andrew completed his education and became a famous lawyer. He moved to a big city, and then his mother seldom saw him. His profession took up all his time.

After some time, Andrew married a girl from a rich family, and after this event, his mother did not see him at all.

Shall I tell you why? I am almost ashamed to say it. This great lawyer had a narrow soul. He was ashamed to confess to his wife his humble beginnings. He feared his wife would be ashamed of his mother. Yet deep down in his heart, Andrew longed for his mother. He had not forgotten her love and care. His longing for his mother finally led him to speak to his wife.

This is what Andrew told his wife. "You know my dear, how servants in the country are different from those in the city. At home we had a faithful maid. When I was sick, she watched over me through many long nights. Had she not cared so faithfully for me, you would never have known me. Up there in the attic, we have a little room, which is not used. If you agree, we will send for dear Mary to come and live with us."

With joy, the young wife gave her consent to the kind plan of her husband. So Andrew sat down and wrote a long letter to his mother. He told her of his wife and how she would not understand that his mother was so plain and simple, and begged her to come to him, but not to tell anyone that she was his mother.

Do you think the mother sent the letter back, outraged? Andrew certainly would have deserved it if she had. A father might have done so, but what would a mother's heart not do in order to be near her son?

She came: a plain little woman. She was introduced to the lawyer's wife: "This is the faithful Mary." From that moment on, Mary lived in the room in the attic.

Humbly, Mary settled down in her new home. When his young wife went out, Andrew sneaked up to his mother's room. Then he would talk to her of his childhood and those hours were the greatest joy of his mother's life.

Nobody else noticed Mary's presence in the house. The dear old Mary remained hidden in her room. Only once, on her arrival, had she been into the beautiful rooms of her son's home. She lived in his home, but only in the attic.

Before I continue this story, I just want to tell you that is how many of us have treated the Holy Spirit of God. He has been with us all the time, but we have locked Him up in our attic. We are too ashamed to bring Him out. Our fancy friends would not understand. Our beautiful wives or husbands will not love us any more, so we have turned out the One Who is like a loving and kind mother to us; the One Who is our Comforter, our Guide; the One Who is supposed to help us when we are weak; the One Who is supposed to teach us all things. We have turned Him out and locked Him in the attic. And because we have done this, we are now left to struggle and suffer. There is no victory in our lives, no wisdom, no Godly knowledge, because, you see, it is the Holy Spirit Who is supposed to teach us all things. While we struggle because of lack of power in our lives, the Holy Spirit sleeps in our attic. What are we going to do next?

I continue Mary's story. True love cannot be deceived. The young wife soon noticed that something was depressing her husband. She asked him, and he told her the truth, that Mary was his mother.

The young wife was so sad and hurt very deeply. She asked her husband, *"How could you believe that I was so narrow-minded?"*

Many of the people you are ashamed to share Jesus Christ with or the Holy Spirit with, are looking for Him. They know something is missing in their lives. So don't think people are so narrow-minded.

Hand in hand, Andrew and his young wife went up to the attic room. His wife took the old woman's hand and pressed her fresh young cheeks against the old one, and said softly, "Mother!!!" The young couple knelt before the old mother and asked for her forgiveness.

Then they led Mary downstairs and the prettiest and sunniest room, in the house, was given her. And from that moment happiness returned into the home.

Once again, I would like to ask you two questions: *"Have you received the Holy Spirit? What will you do with the Holy Spirit?"*

Receiving Him is welcoming Him into your life, into your home, giving Him His rightful place as the One Who is called to take you by the hand, and teach you all things, guide you into all truth. He must have His rightful place in your lives or else you can never have the victory God intended for you to have.

The Bible says, "As many as received Him, He gave them power to become the sons of God." This is the beginning of the Christian life. It begins with receiving and not giving, and continues like that to the end. The father gives, the child accepts. For our lives to have meaning we must put the Holy Spirit in His rightful place. If we fail to do that we will never taste true victory in this world.

One of the most powerful acts of the Holy Spirit was the virgin birth. The birth of our Lord Jesus was a miracle.

> The Angel of God appeared to Mary, and told her these words, "Do not be afraid, Mary, you have found favour with God. You will be with child and give birth to a Son, and you are to call His Name, Jesus. He will be great and will be called the Son of the Most High."
>
> Mary asked, "How will this be, since I am a virgin?"
>
> The Angel answered, "The Holy Spirit will come upon you, and the power of the Most High will overshadow you. So the Holy One to be born will be called the Son of God. (Luke 1: 30, 34-35)

Many people doubt the *virgin birth*. This has robbed them of God's blessing. For me, this passage of scripture has established me for ever in the kingdom of God. I totally trust the Holy Spirit. If my Lord and Saviour Jesus, Who was at the right hand of God, trusted the Holy Spirit to bring Him down to earth and conceive Him in the womb of a virgin, then for me there is no reason why I cannot trust the Holy Spirit totally. Try trusting Him and see what He will do. For many of you, men and women, who desire to conceive, this is the Person Who is the giver of life. No one can stop the Holy Spirit, when He decides to move.

The Bible says in Psalm 104: 30, "When you [God] send your Spirit, they are created." Wherever the Spirit of God is there is creativity, because He is the giver of life. He is the One that creates the words that come from our lips, the words that are conceived by the Word of God.

I want to encourage you to know the Giver of life Himself.

Receive the Holy Spirit.

How do I receive him?

Invite Jesus into your life as the Lord of your life. When Jesus is the Lord of your life the Holy Spirit also comes. Develop your relationship with the Holy Spirit by talking to Him and sharing things with Him as you would share with a spouse. You will be amazed to see what you will discover. The Holy Spirit is a *real person. God bless you as you pursue this relationship.*

Your prayer

Sweet Holy Spirit! I have read about You. I never knew Who you were or that I could have a personal relationship with You. Today I know for sure that you are a Person and that you are my Teacher and my friend. Take me by the hand and lead me. I don't even know which way to go or what to do, but I belive and trust that from to day You will lead and guide me in all my ways in Jesus name. Thank You for loving me and caring for me and from today teach me how to love You in Jesus name I pray. Amen.

Chapter Two

Woman, You Are Not Infertile

"Woman, you are infertile." Who said that to you? Can't conceive, can't reproduce, barren, sterile, incapable? Who said those words to you? The Bible says: -"*You can through Christ who straightens you.*" For this is what God says to you: *"Be fruitful and multiply and replenish the earth. (Genesis 1: 28)*

Who then is this God that said these words to you? The Bible says, "He is the one who created the heavens and the earth and everything in it, with the words of His mouth."

By faith we understand that the universe was formed at God's command so that what is seen was not made out of what was visible. (Hebrew 11: 3)

After God had created the universe, God again decided to create man in His own image after His likeness.

> Then God said, "Let us make man in our image, in our likeness and let them rule over the fishes of the sea and birds of the air, over the livestock, over all the earth, and over all the creatures that move along the ground." So God created man in his own image, in the image of God he created him; male and female he created them. God blessed them, and said to them, "Be fruitful and increase in number; fill the earth and subdue it. (Genesis 1: 26-28)

This is God's perfect will for creating man. (Most times when you read the word man in the Bible it is applicable to both sexes - male and female.)

How did God create man?

He the master potter, the Lord God formed the first man from the dust of the ground and breathed into his nostrils the breath of life and the man became a living being. (Genesis 2: 7) Here in the account of creation we see that God first created a man - a male.

God creates the woman (Genesis 2: 21-23)

Then in the second stage of creation we see what God did next.

> So the Lord God caused the man to fall into a deep sleep; and while he was sleeping, he took one of the man's ribs and closed up the place with flesh. Then the Lord God made a woman from the rib he had taken out of the man, he brought her to the man. (Genesis 2: 21-23)

This is what the Holy Spirit taught me. How many of us know you cannot create a fully grown woman with just a rib? This is what the Lord did. He made the woman from the dust of the earth as He created the man.

What is the meaning of "to make"?

It means to assemble or prepare, especially by putting various ingredients together. God used the saliva of His mouth and the dust of the earth to make her and He made her special.

When God made the woman He took time to make her skilfully. When you look at the reproductive organs of woman you will know that this is the work of a skilful God who knew exactly what He had planned and what to do in order to accomplish His plans. Looking at the female reproductive organs you see a most wonderful piece of workmanship done by Almighty God.

Starting from the vagina, you come to the cervix and from the cervix, you come to the uterus or the womb which is where the foetus grows for nine months. The womb is lined by the endometrium, which is a specialised type of tissue that undergoes changes during the menstrual cycle. You then find the ovaries which contain the eggs and also the Fallopian tube which transports the egg into the womb. Each piece of the female reproductive anatomy is designed to work in harmony so as to accomplish a specific purpose which is the production of a child. What of the ribs God took from the man? God put the ribs in her ovaries.

What are ovaries?

They are a pair of almond-shaped glands situated on both sides of the womb, immediately below the Fallopian tube opening. The ovaries consist of numerous egg-producing follicles. The ovaries do not only produce eggs but also the female sex hormones - oestrogen and progesterone - as well as a small amount of the male sex hormone, testosterone.

God leaves his signature

Medical science can testify that women produce a small amount of the male sex hormone, testosterone, in their ovaries. Why? This is because the reproductive part of her came from the ribs of the man which God put in the ovaries. No man produces the female sex hormone, oestrogen, in their bodies.

When Adam saw Eve, he said these words about her beauty: "This is now bone of my bones and flesh of my flesh, she shall be called woman for she was taken out of man." She was a man but she had a womb. God had created her to carry his children in her womb. Therefore, for those who are curious, and are wondering why women produce testosterone in their bodies, the reason is that part of her came from the man. The Word of God is true. When God created the man and made the woman, He commanded them to be, "fruitful and increase in number and fill the earth," which means the only way the earth can be replenished is by multiplication or increase.

Father, we praise you, for you have wonderfully and skilfully created a woman to fulfil a specific purpose; only you, God, could have done these things - we give you praise for you, Almighty God, are exalted above the heavens.

Who is like the Lord our God? Who stoops down to look on the heavens and the earth?

What is to stoop? It means to bend the body forwards and downwards, sometimes simultaneously bending the knees. It also means to lower oneself morally. The seat of God almighty is so high that in order to behold the things in the heaven and on the earth, He has to humble himself, that is He has to stoop. Then the purpose of that stooping is revealed; it is that He may raise the poor and lift the needy. Then finally it moves on to say, *"he settles the barren woman..."* God then again stoops to crown womanhood with motherhood.

The God who dwells in the heavens above had stooped through His love and grace in His only begotten son Jesus Christ, in order that He might lift the needy. As He approached the ultimate depths in this stooping, He once again declared His intentions: "to settle the barren woman in her home as a happy mother of children." (Psalms 113: 6-9) Praise the Lord.

Father, I praise you for stooping just to bless me. I thank you for Your words that say I'm a mother of all living. I am created in the pattern of Eve - she was the mother of all living; she was not barren so I am not barren either.

Father, thank-you for creating me as a woman to fulfil your plans and purpose on this earth. I thank you because this will surely come to pass in Jesus' Name.

However, for one reason or another, we know that God's original intention has changed. In the world today many women have become infertile for one reason or another. The word infertile hurts and is frightening to the woman involved. To her infertility strikes at her very womanhood, robbing her of joy and peace, and bringing an emptiness that words cannot describe. We cannot fully understand the extent of the pain the woman goes through, except if we ourselves have experienced it. My mother used to say, "You cannot tell where a man's shoes are hurting unless you are wearing his shoes." And so it is with this issue of infertility.

The first time I read about infertility, I was shocked to read about what women were being told concerning their fertility. Some were told by specialist fertility doctors that they would not be able to conceive in their lifetime.

I was not satisfied with this and I decided to take it up with God. I knew from reading the Bible and from walking with God personally that nothing is impossible with God. I also noticed in the Bible that every woman who had a fertility problem later conceived and bore children. I also remember Psalms 113: 9, which says: "He settles the barren women in her home as a happy mother of children. "

For every woman the greatest fulfilment of her life comes through being able to meet her call as a mother, to bring forth a child into the world. The Bible says: "The call of God is without repentance," which means that God has not changed His mind about every woman being a mother of children. That's why He created you - to be a "mother of all the living". (Genesis 3: 20)

Bereavement

During my research for this book I read about a woman who was told by her specialist that she could not have children and this is what she said: "Each time my period came I went through a bereavement, a time of great disappointment, mourning, a loss; I became empty and devastated." This is God's promise to any woman who feels this way through His Son, Jesus Christ: "Although you are alone today with your arms empty, tomorrow you will be able to say:

The children born during my bereavement will yet say in my hearing 'This place is too small for us, give us more space to live in.' Then I will say in my heart, 'Who bore me these? I was bereaved and barren, I was exiled and rejected, who brought these up? I was left all alone but these - where have they come from?' (Isaiah 49: 20-21)"

God is telling you today, woman, your days of barrenness are over, your days of emptiness are over. The times of being robbed of the joy of motherhood is over; your arms will now be filled with joy from nursing your own children in Jesus' name - you will say, *"I was left alone, but all these children, where did they come from?"* God will bring His Word to pass in your life in Jesus' name. Then you will declare with joy in your heart:

It is good to give thanks and praise to the Lord and make music to your name, O Most High, to proclaim your love in the morning and your faithfulness at night ... (Psalms 92: 1-2)

When those children start running all over you, you will be so full of joy that you will not even remember all the pain and suffering you have gone through. For this is God's promise to you.

"Then you will know that I am the Lord, those who hope in me will not be disappointed." (Isaiah 49: 23) God sees your pain and desire and wants you to know that in Christ all things are possible.

I love you today and I want you to know that Jesus loves you. I feel your pain because Jesus feels it. I care for you because Jesus cares about you. He has commanded me to write this book to give you His words and His commands.

These words are not mine but the words of our Lord Jesus Christ. He wants His beloved women to know that He loves them, that He is the one who created you, the one who died to redeem you from the power of sin by shedding His blood on the Cross of Calvary. He is the one who loves you with an everlasting love - Today He says to you, "I have given you all the children you need. In you I have put a seed and that seed will come forth - That's why, in Genesis 3: 15, I promised the woman that her seed will crush the enemies' head." When that child comes God will use that child to destroy the works of darkness. You have a seed in you and God needs that seed. You are part of God's plan to accomplish His purpose on the earth. Woman the seed in you must come forth - God needs that child in you. Please believe this. I have written down everything that my Lord Jesus Christ has commanded me to write to His beautiful women, because I know that His Word leads to eternal life and deliverance in all areas of our lives. Jesus loves you so much; you are beautiful to Him. The Bible says you are fearfully and wonderfully made (Psalms 139: 14) And in Christ you are fruitful.

Hurts and pains

God sees all your pains and He knows about all your tears and He says these words to you: *"Weeping may endure for the night but joy comes in the morning."* Stop crying, wipe your tears, for in Christ all things are possible to those that believe. If you embrace the truths written in this book and apply them, you will find God to be true. You have more than enough in this book to help every woman conceive in Jesus' name, why? Because the Word of God is not void of power neither can it fail to accomplish what it has been sent to do.

Walking uprightly

No good thing does he withhold from those whose walk is blameless. (Psalms 84: 11)

In the time of Herod, king of Judea, there was a priest named Zachariah who belong to the priestly division of Abijah; his wife Elizabeth was also a descendant of Aaron. Both of them were upright in the sight of God, observing all the Lord's commandments and regulations blamelessly. But they had no children because Elizabeth was barren and they were well on in years. (Luke 1: 5-7)

An angel of the Lord appeared to him and said to him, "Do not be afraid, Zachariah, your prayers have been heard. Your wife Elizabeth will bear you a son and you are to give him the name John. (Luke 1: 13)

"After this, his wife Elizabeth became pregnant. When it was time for her to have her baby, she gave birth to a son. Her neighbours and relations heard that the Lord had shown her great mercy and they shared her joy. (Luke 1: 57-58) What is mercy? Mercy is:- an act of divine compassion or a blessing or a fortunate circumstance. God changed her circumstance, changed her story and put a song in her mouth.

Why is this so? Because this couple walked upright, and were blameless before God. They never stopped praying, never stopped believing, never stopped trusting God to fulfil His promise to those who put their trust in Him. Even after many years, God still blessed them because no upright person will be denied any good thing, no matter how long it takes - light will always shine for the upright.

Rights and absolute rights

I read in a book where a doctor wrote this words: -"We all have rights but the right to have a baby is not one of them. It is a worthy goal, a pleasure, even a privilege but not an absolute right," he concludes. I totally disagree with this writer because in Christ Jesus the right to have a child is absolute. The Bible says: "Through a knowledge of God we are given all things that pertain unto life and godliness. (2 Peter 1: 3) The Bible says we are given all things which means all the things that we need, including children. God has no choice but to bless you with children if you are walking obediently with Him because God is not a man to lie to anyone. Whatever He promises He brings to pass. The Bible says all the promises of God in Christ Jesus are "yes" and Amen. It clearly says there is nothing like "no" in all the promises God made in His Son, Jesus Christ. (2 Corinthians 2: 20)

Giving us the desires of our hearts

"May he give you the desires of your hearts." (Psalms 20: 4) The Bible says that He gives us the desires of our heart. The desire to have children is built in by God - that's why it never goes away, that's why you are very determined to conceive. Even at a very tender age, girls have been nurtured with motherly tendencies; for instance, I have watched my four-year-old daughter playing mummy and baby with her doll. Where did she get that desire to be a mum? It is God in-built, it is God who gives us the desires of our heart - and until that desire is met, we are never fulfilled. The Bible says a barren womb is never satisfied.

But in Christ we can find rest, just trusting Him and casting our cares upon Him for nothing is too hard for Him. "With God all things are possible." (Matthew 19 : 26)

Authority and command

The Holy Spirit taught me about infertility in one interesting area that of the place of command and authority.

What is command?

To command means to direct authoritatively. Who gives this command? Someone in authority always gives a command to someone under that authority. That command once given must be carried out without any questions asked. Any question if necessary may be asked after the command has been carried out.

A person in authority is described as an individual cited as or appealed to as an expert. A person in authority has the power to require and receive submission, the right to expect obedience, power to influence or to command; a right can be granted by somebody in authority, for instance people in command, a person in command, a government body in command, From this dictionary description, we can see God as the highest authority requiring our obedience and submission. God as the creator of the universe gave this command to man - "Be fruitful and increase over the earth." God therefore authorised man to multiple and increase on the earth.

A commanding authority must as a rule provide all the essential equipment needed to enable its subjects to carry out the command given without hardship or difficulty. Even the Bible asks this question in I Corinthians 9 : 7: "Who serves as a soldier at his own expense?" The answer is nobody. When a nation sends out men to war it must provide their fighting men with guns, bullet, food, warm clothes, uniforms, medical care and everything the soldiers require for the successful completion of that assignment. The same applies in the spiritual realm, since God is the One who created man and commanded man to multiply, He has no choice but to provide man with everything man needs in order to accomplish this command.

As you can see man had no choice in this matter. God commands us to multiply and increase, so God must provide the woman with all she needs to fulfil this assignment, the right vagina, womb, Fallopian tubes, ovaries - all her reproductive organs must be functioning properly. If any thing is missing, God, as the commanding authority, has the power and the ability to fix it. You may say, "Well, God was only speaking to Adam and Eve." No, when God spoke to them, you and I were in seed form in the body of these people. "Adam named his wife Eve because she would become the mother of all the living." (Genesis 3: 20) In one woman, Eve, God put eggs enough to produce millions of children.

The mystery of creation is this. A woman gets pregnant. If the fertilised egg is a female embryo, then after twenty-one days it starts to develop within itself a group of cells which specialise and become her ovaries. Initially only a group of one hundred cells. The primitive ovary moves into position within the embryo and starts to grow. At their peak the ovaries will contain a few million eggs and the numbers are starting to decline, even before birth. The surviving cells are immature and they need to wait patiently for thirteen years or more - until the girl reaches puberty. At this point, only half a million or less will still be present of which some four or five hundred will be released, and only a *handful* of these will ever be fertilised and grow into babies. Why all these eggs if all you need is between five and twenty since some women may only normally have up to twenty children? The answer is clear.

On the day of Creation God created one woman. In that woman he put millions of eggs - enough to populate the whole world. Every other woman born into the world was to be in the pattern of that one woman. The mystery of this is that nobody needs to help the baby in the womb to grow eggs or ovaries as everything is automatic. Once more we see the potential of the Creator working in the life of every woman on earth.

The Bible says it is, "through one man that God created all nations of men [women]." (Acts 17: 26) Even Eve was taken from the man. God works using potential as a principle - in one man He packaged the seed to populate the whole world. Medically it is a fact that a man produces in his testes about ten million sperm cells a day. This figure alone is enough to populate the whole world in just six months, yet all that is needed to make a baby is just a single sperm. So there is no doubt that all human beings were in Adam the day God created him. The Bible account is to be relied upon totally - from one man God created the whole nation of men (Acts 17: 26) Right now all the children you desire are locked up inside you; you need the Word of God, spoken out of your mouth in faith (trust) to bring those children out, according to the power that works within you.

The best specialist in the world may have told you, "It is impossible, you can't conceive." Well, whose report will you believe? God says "you can" man says "you can't." Choose today for yourself what you will believe. Remember this command -*"Be fruitful, increase and*

20

replenish the earth. " (Genesis 1: 28). This is God's command to you. For with God all things are possible. (Matthew 19: 26)

Effects and the importance of God's commands

God's Word cannot be bound

One thing about God's commands are that they are boundless - the Bible says "God's commands are boundless." (Psalms 119: 96) What does boundless mean? It means His command cannot be limited by any circumstances or any lack. He who created the universe and created man, gave man the command to "multiply." Nothing in your life is supposed to stop you from fulfilling this call. No lack is enough, be it lack of vagina or womb or Fallopian tube, congenital disorder nothing is supposed to stop you. Where any lack exists you have every right to ask God to meet that need. You may ask where can I see God? God himself gave us this open invitation: "Come boldly before the throne of mercy that you may receive mercy and find grace to help you in your time of need. (Hebrews 4: 16) God even went further and invited us to come and reason with Him. "Come now, let us reason together," says the Lord. (Isaiah 1: 18) This is an open invitation from the creator of the universe to His children. God invites us to come and reason with Him. God is ready to talk to you any day, any time, anywhere, if you are ready. If you are sincere and desire the truth, God will surely meet with you and reason with you. He will answer your deepest questions and solve the problems nobody could solve for you. He will give you the desires of your heart in Jesus' name. Remember God's commands are boundless.

All God's commands are trustworthy

All God's commands are trustworthy. (Psalms 119: 86) This means you can totally rely on them, totally depend on them, totally put your confidence in them, because they are honest and true. God alone will never lie to you or deceive you.

God's commands give wisdom (Psalms 119: 98)

All God's commands will make you wiser than your enemies. (Psalms 119: 98) for God's commands are ever with you. When infertility stares you in the face, you can say to it, "Because of God's command I am going to have that child because God is giving me the wisdom and understanding to

21

hold on to His command. I am going to defeat you in Jesus' name because God's Word makes me wiser than you, greater is He that is in me than he that is in the world." Speak these words clearly and loudly when these "Can't" words start to come to you. Tell them, "I can and surely will because God said '*I can do all things through Christ who gives me strength.*'" (Philippians 4: 13

Scientific background

The dictionary defines infertility as the inability to produce offspring. For a pregnancy to occur, the woman must be healthy and be ovulating and evidence of this is having her monthly period. The man must also be producing healthy sperms. Sexual intercourse must also be taking place for one of the millions of sperms ejaculated by the man to reach the woman's Fallopian tubes and fertilise the egg. The egg will fertilise in the Fallopian tube before finally embedding itself in the womb. Infertility is suggested only if a couple has had unprotected intercourse for one year without a pregnancy. Listed below are some reasons why a pregnancy could fail to occur in the female - damage to the Fallopian-tubes, blocked Fallopian tubes, (where the tubes are often removed because of congenital defeats), hormone problems, ovulation problems, etc. It is estimated that around 100 million couples are affected by infertility world-wide. Thirty per cent of infertility is due to male factors, thirty per cent to female factors and in the remaining forty per cent the cause of infertility could be attributed to both partners.

Chapter Three

Congential Disorders

Congenital disorders (that which a woman is born with).

Ovarian problems

Some women have been born without ovaries or ovaries that contain no eggs; no amount of medical treatment can overcome this.

Hormone problems

These occur where a woman's pituitary gland does not produce LH and FSH - because she lacks a working copy of the genes that cause the hormones to be built.

Turner's disease

This is an abnormality that affects the chromosomes. Most women are born with forty-five chromosomes instead of forty-six. This means they are missing one X chromosome. Since the normal complement for women is XX, some women could have an extra X chromosome making them XXX. This disease causes retarded development of the sexual organs which results in an absence of menstruation. Any woman suffering from this disorder remains infertile.

Congenital womb problems

Some women are born with wombs that are the wrong shape and in some cases the womb may be totally absent. In other cases there could be a left and right uterus each having its own cervix and vagina. Incorrect formation of the womb can lead to infertility.

Fallopian tube problems

Some women are born with tubes that are the wrong shape or they might have being removed in surgery, due to an ectopic pregnancy or cancer of the uterus or some other reason; there may have been total or partial removal of the reproductive organs. I have included them in the congenital groups as those needing a creative miracle. This is because though born with these parts they have lost them through a hysterectomy. What is a hysterectomy?

Hysterectomy

This is the removal of the womb. It may be performed to remove the womb or the cervix or even the ovaries. Causes for these include cancer of the womb or cervix, fibroid or ovarian cancer. In other cases it is performed to relieve heavy bleeding or the reason may be a condition called endometriosis where fragments of the uterus lining occur in the pelvic area and do not respond to treatment; a severally damaged uterus could be removed in a hysterectomy.

Testicular Feminisation syndrome

This is a rare, inherited condition where a person may have all the external appearance of a female, but the affected individual is genetically a male with internal testes. This is a form of intersex. The cause of this syndrome is a defective response of the body tissue to the male sex hormone, testosterone, even though a normal male level of the hormone is produced. People affected by this syndrome appear to be girls throughout their childhood.

At puberty they develop normal female secondary sexual characteristics but menstruation does not start because there is no uterus and the vagina is short and blind-ended. In most cases it will not be detected until puberty when investigation is carried out to find out why menstruation has not started. At this stage, a chromosome analysis is performed which will reveal that the girl has normal male chromosomal status. A blood test will indicate male levels of testosterone (male sex hormones) in her. If a girl is found to have an inguinal hernia or swelling in her labia that turns out to be testes, an operation will be carried out by a doctor to remove the testes because of the risk of testicular cancer. An affected individual can never be fertile, but can lead an otherwise normal life as a woman. Oestrogen drugs can also be used to treat such individuals to create more female sex hormones in their body.

I have decided to leave this open for anybody who may face this problem; you alone can decide what you want God to do for you. If you want to remain a female or if you feel within you, that you are a man, then, when you make that decision, you will be able to ask God for the creative miracle you want. Be sure of this, God wants to make you whole and to bless you if you will dare to believe Him. God loves you.

Atresia

This is where a woman is born without a body closure. A woman could be born with a partial or incomplete vagina or there could be a blockage to the external opening of the vagina by an unperforated hymen. While writing this book, I spoke to my brother in Christ, Doctor Sola Oso, about this issue and he told me only a few women are born this way. I also discovered that many women who face this problem have gone to fertility clinics to help them fulfil their desire to have children. If you are one of these women, Jesus wants you to know that He loves you. He has sent His Word to bring you hope and total victory; you can have that child. He will wipe away all your tears and bring you joy and peace. He will meet you at the point of your need. Remember when anyone says to you, "you can't" tell them *"I can, and I will not be on my own beacause I have the help of Christ who strengthens me."*

If there is any other congenital defect I have not mentioned - the same prescription from the Word of God will work in all cases. God bless you. I love you.

No matter what you have gone through today, I bring you good news. Jesus loves you, He cares about you, He feels all your pains and has promised to restore to you all the wasted years. He wants you to know you can have that baby; you can do all things through Christ who strengthens you. (Philippians 4: 13) All things means all things, for with God all things are possible. (Luke 1: 37)

What the Bible offers - creative miracles

A congenital disorder is something which is existing or dating back to the time of birth. God wants you to know this, no matter the congenital disorder you may face He does not blame you for it, neither does He take the blame for it, that is why He sent Jesus to come into the world and shed His blood on the Cross to save man. In shedding His blood He also destroyed the works of darkness which is what this disorder is all about. Congenital disorder is not of God. The Bible says "every good and perfect gift comes from God, the father of the heavenly lights who does not change like shifting shadows." (James 1: 17) This means until this earth passes away God remains the giver of every good and perfect gift.

God is not the author of evil - the Bible says God cannot be tempted by evil nor does he tempt anyone. (James 1: 13) Today you need a creative miracle in your life and I want to introduce you to the great

25

creator, proving once and for all that Jesus Christ is who He claims to be. The Bible says,

> In the beginning was the Word, and the Word was with God, and the Word was God. (John 1: 1-4)

Through him all things were made, without him; nothing was made that has been made. Nothing was made and nothing can be made without Jesus. Jesus is the great Creator. He alone can meet all your needs from the day you are born to the day you die and return to be with Him in glory. He will, if you ask Him, present himself to you in the natural and spiritual realm as your creator and bring deliverance from every difficulty as you behold Him for yourself for who He is.

Jesus' blessing is on every marriage

The first institution Jesus created after He created the earth was the institution of marriage. The first creative miracle He performed when He started His earthly ministry was at a marriage ceremony proving once and for all that He will not joke about any issue that affects the purpose, the joy and happiness of the institution of marriage.

Under the leadership of the Holy Spirit we take a journey to the Book of John in the Bible.

Jesus at a wedding (John 2: 1- 11)

Here we read of Jesus in a marriage

> On the third day, a wedding took place at Cana in Galilee. Jesus' mother was there and Jesus and his disciples had also being invited to the wedding. When the wine was gone, Jesus' mother said to him, "They have no more wine." (John 2: 1-3)

Here was an emergency in the middle of a wedding party - maybe it was in the evening when all the shops were closed. What will this couple do now? Oh, give praise to God for He is good, and His mercies endure forever. Jesus was around, this couple were wise; they had invited Jesus, the great creator of heaven and earth. I pray today every couple will learn to invite Jesus into their home and in everything they plan to do. Everyday I personally acknowledge Him in my home, commit

26

my husband, children and work into His hands. He has been faithful to me.

Immediately Jesus was told they had no wine, our Lord moved into action. Nearby stood six stone water jars, the kind used by the Jews for ceremonial washing - each holding from twenty to thirty gallons of water. Jesus said to the servants, "Fill the jars with water," so they filled them to the brim. Then He told them, "Now draw some out and take it to the master of the banquet.

They did so and the master of the banquet tasted the water that had been turned into wine. He did not realise where it had come from, though the servants who had drawn the water knew. Then he called the bridegroom aside and said to him, "Everyone brings out the choice wine first and then the cheaper wine after the guests have had too much to drink, but you have saved the best till now. (John 2: 6-10)

Following this miracle to the end, your faith will be lifted and you will be able to receive all you need as you behold Jesus as the great creator. You will also see how easy it is for Him to create because He alone is the great creator.

First the six water pots were filled to the brim by those servants; there was no chance of cheating here. Jesus could not slip anything into a pot already filled to the brim. Secondly, we cannot even say when the miracle took place because we do not hear Him saying any long prayers or even going near the pots or saying any words. The first thing we hear Him say is to command the servant to fill the pot with water, the next is to fetch the water and take it to the master of the feast. We only get a confirmation from the master of the feast that the water was now choice wine - the best of them all. The amazing thing about this miracle is that the master of the feast did not even know that it was water because he was not there when everything took place but he confirmed that it was choice wine and the very best. Our Lord dispensing with all natural laws does in one moment what normally takes years to do. I actually took the time to find out about the process of vine planting through to wine making to help you appreciate the greatness of our great creator, Jesus Christ. I also want you to know that the turning of water into wine in an instant is a creative miracle.

Wine

During my research I came across the best wine in the world today, a choice wine that can be compared with the choice wine Jesus created in an instant that day in Cana. This is the most sought after wine in the world. It is called Château d'Yquem. It is drunk by royalty. Prince Charles raised a glass of Château d'Yquem to Princess Diana on their wedding day. It is used world-wide at state dinners and parties. Two hundred and fifty bottles of this wine was bottled in 1788 and bought by Thomas Jefferson in the same year when he was America's ambassador to France. One bottle of this wine was sold for £36,000 pounds in December 1986 at Christies of London (*Readers Digest*, September 1988). This wine can match up a bit to the wine Jesus created in an instant on that wedding day in Cana, Galilee. I have used this example to show the similar ties between the natural process of planting through to wine making and that of a human being from conception to birth.

The process

Planting

You need a vineyard to plant the vine and for Château d'Yquem they have an incomparable site on top of one of the highest hills in an area where the soil is a unique mixture of small pebbles and clay. Normally the vine enjoys a drained soil, little rainfall and a warm humid atmosphere.

Each year the fruit-bearing shoots must be pruned since the fruit is borne on shoots from the previous year's wood. A vine needs four years to develop sufficiently to bear fruit for wine making.

A baby

In comparison, all it takes is thirtyeight - forty weeks for a new baby to be born. The pruning stage of the grapes can be compared to the ante-natal care a mother goes through during the period of pregnancy, eating the right food, exercising the right way to enable her to bring forth a healthy baby.

Picking the grapes

To pick the grapes to make this wine, about thirty people are lead by a team leader. He stands at the end of each vine row, inspecting the grapes as each member carefully selects the right grapes, each hand-picked carefully. The grapes picked must not only be ripe but to make this wine, the grapes picked must have what they call grey rot. "It is not enough that grapes be ripe to make this wine they must be nicely rotted as well." Imagine choice wine made out of carefully selected, rotten grapes, each specially hand-picked. Yet this is how the most sort-after wine in the world is made from grey rot grapes.

A baby

The picking of the grapes can be compared to the hospital visits for scans, and check-ups to see how the baby is developing and the shopping trips to buy all mummy's and baby's needs when the baby is born.

Veraison

This is the stage just before the full ripeness of the grapes; they have reached their maximum size and weight, but are not completely ripe. From this stage the sugar content increases and the acidity decreases; between this period of *veraison* and ripeness, the appearances of the skin hardly changes and this makes it very difficult to judge the right time of picking. Nowadays, picking is determined by analysis of the grape samples in the laboratory.

A baby

Glory to God. This stage can be compared to the growth of the foetus. By the thirty-second week of pregnancy all the internal organs of the foetus are fully formed and matured, but the baby is not ready to be born. During this period fat is being deposited under the baby's skin so that it looks plumper. While all this is happening God is watching over that baby in the womb.

Unlike the vineyard owner, who has to analyse the grapes in His laboratory, God has already set the time of birth according to the Bible. (Acts 17: 26)

The crushing

This process does not end in the vineyard; the grapes are taken to be crushed and crushed as quickly as possible to extract the juice. In the days of our Lord Jesus Christ, this was even harder work because no machinery was available - grapes were either crushed by the tread of bare feet, or heavy stones, or by mules, but today we have modern machinery to make this easier to do. The grapes are gently crushed without cracking open the pips whose oil would taint the wine. The resultant pulp goes into a press which squeezes out a cascade of pure juice.

A baby

This can be compared to the contractions at labour; this affects the walls of the uterus, as marked by discomfort experienced as the contractions grow stronger and the frequency intensifies to propel the baby out of the womb.

The press

This instrument was used since ancient times to extract as much juice as possible from already crushed grapes and fruits. Force was originally provided by heavy stone, feet, levers and, finally, screws turned by men and animals but later hydraulic force was used. More recently, the airbag has been developed. This contraption consists of perforated stainless steel containing a deflated rubber bag. Once filled with crushed grapes, the bag is inflated and the pulp pressed against the perforation through which the juice escapes into a container placed beneath the stainless steel sieve.

A baby

This can be compared to the final push before the baby is born into the world; here the mother will need all her strength for the big push to bring the baby into the world.

Vessel

A vessel is any hollow receptacle for holding liquid and can be of any shape, and made of any material. When applied to wine making, a vessel refers to a receptacle which will hold a must of wine and can be closed in such a manner that wine will not suffer contamination or spoilage. It can be in a barrel, cast, jar, tank, etc.

A baby

This can be compared to the womb, which is the hollow muscular organ of the female reproductive organ. This is where the fertilised egg embeds itself and the embryo develops. In the womb is the amniotic fluid, which protects the baby from infection. The environment of the womb makes it conducive for the healthy growth of the foetus.

Fermentation and fermentation chamber

Fermentation is the magical, natural process by which yeast breaks down the grapes' sugar into desirable alcohol which stays in the wine while unwanted carbon dioxide floats hissing away. Treated carelessly, the yeast can die, giving not wine but vinegar. Through long weeks of fragmentation, the skilled wine-maker watches and makes adjustments, like a nurse tending an incubated baby.

A baby

Glory to God, when that baby is in the womb, we will keep on believing God that the baby will not come out prematurely, for God watches over the life of that baby. He has set the right time for it to be born. The Bible says in Ecclesiastes 3: 2 that there is a time to be born.

Filtering

This is a method of passing wine through a medium with pores small enough to remove suspended matter but not fine enough to remove the molecules of bacchant, colour or flavour. There are different ways and methods of doing this.

A baby

This method can be compared to the placenta that develops in the womb, when a woman is pregnant; linking the blood supply of the mother and the baby, it acts as an organ of respiration and excretion for the foetus; it aids in the transportation of oxygen from the mother's circulation into the foetus' circulation and removes the waste products from the foetus by systemic re-circulation into the maternal blood, for excretion by her lungs and kidneys.

Fining

A wine must have clarity and brilliance to have eye appeal and be attractive. Properly racked wines nearly always go bright naturally after standing for a while in a cool place. Some wines however, persistently remain hazy even after several rackings and it is these wines that have to be subjected to other means of clarification. This is where fining comes in, it is done in these ways.

[A]   By addition of an agent that causes precipitation

31

or physical fining.

[B]   By purification with the use of an agent or chemical fining.

Maturation

This is the process of ageing wine until it is in peak condition and ready for drinking. Although it is well-known that all wines improve during the process of maturing, the causes and chemical reactions are still not completely understood. During this stage of maturing, malic and succinic acids are reduced to esters (an ethereal salt); acetic acid is formed in very small quantities; some tannin is oxidised; there is a reduction of fusel oils to acids and aldehydes; acetal, which is very aromatic and forms an important part of the bouquet is produced from a combination of the aldehydes and alcohol. Effects to speed up maturing by ionic exchanges, by oxidising and through the use of other agents - electrical discharge, exposure to the sun, heating - have all failed to produce the quality of age.

A baby

While reading my Bible, it was interesting to read in Isaiah that the Lord Almighty prepares a feast for His people using aged wine, so God knows more about this maturing phase than we do. He will give you a fully matured baby, not a quickly processed one, in Jesus' mighty name. (Isaiah 27: 2-3)

Bottling

Wine is also aged in bottles. Some wine needs at least a year in the bottle for the further interaction of the alcohol in order to produce elders and esters and develop bouquet and flavour. The wines also mellow and improve in character while in the bottle. Others may require several years in the bottle to reach their peak. Full-bodied and heavy dessert wines require even longer and may remain in the bottle for fifteen years or more before reaching our tables. I suggest that you should buy a book on vineyards and wine-making to learn more about the process. The processes I listed are just a few of those involved to get a bottle of wine onto our tables. It takes years of hard work - and yet our Lord did this in one instant. I have compared the process of wine-making and the birth of a child to show you the similarities and prove to you that wine making is a creative miracle just like childbirth.

Jesus makes it look easy

Our Lord Jesus set aside those stages of wine-making in an instant through the operation of another law not known or understood by the ordinary man; He made water become wine, because He alone is the great creator: "...all things were made by him and for him and without him was not anything made that was made." (John 1: 13)

Many people may say: "How does this wine-making business concern me? I don't need wine. I need a baby, I don't have a womb or vagina, or a Fallopian tubes etc., so how can I have a baby?" This is a good question, but by going through the entire process of wine-making especially from the vine stage when grapes are planted through to full maturation, you have seen how long and hard it is by physical means to get a bottle of wine onto our tables. No choice wine can get to you in less than ten years from vine planting to maturation - Our Lord did that in an instant, without even saying a Word, He turned ordinary water into red bubbling wine. His turning water into wine was a creative miracle. He is also able to create all your needs in an instant to help you conceive and bear a child.

I am not saying He is going to make a baby fall down from heaven into your laps. No, you also have a part to play.

Note when He turned the water to wine, obedience was involved. He told the servants, "fill the six water pots to the brim." They obeyed Him. "Fetch the water and take it to the master of the feast." They again obeyed His commands. God will never do a man's work. Anything man can do, God will let man do. What man cannot do, God will then do for man by miraculous working power. This is because the power of miraculous working will not violate nature; miracles are beyond the scope of nature, producing results which nature alone is incapable of producing.

God will create any missing part of the reproductive organs you may need to help you conceive. I know He will do that for you but you will have to carry that pregnancy for the full term; the baby will not drop into your laps from heaven.

God has fixed the natural laws, and they are what normally work but all the natural laws are subject to Him. Sometimes He intercedes and uses His power to achieve the impossible, if he desires something, God is not bound or limited by natural laws.

In demonstrating His creative and all-transforming power He puts aside ten to twenty years of the time it takes to make a good wine, and in an instant creates choice wine in abundance. No wonder the Bible says He is able to do, "immeasurably more than all we can ask or imagine according to the power at work within us." (Ephesians 3: 20)

The Bible says He can do more than you or I can ask for. So what are you asking for? He is able to do more than you can ask for. When Mary came to our Lord Jesus and said, "they have no wine" (John 2: 3) even she herself did not know what our Lord Jesus was going to do. So whatever you ask, He will exceed that.

Imagine - what can you imagine? A baby, a new womb, a vagina, Fallopian tubes? What do you crave for most, what is it that makes you feel that if only you had it, you will be able to have a baby? Well, the Bible says He is able to do more than you can imagine - which in effect means God is able to give you more than that which you desire, even more than what you have imagined.

The couple in question did not imagine that by the end of their wedding day, they would have surplus choice wine after their guests had left. As we can all clearly see, this couple were poor, they were just managing to make ends meet. But they were very wise by deciding to marry and do the right thing before God. Above all, they had the wisdom to invite Jesus to their marriage.

Super abundant blessing flows

Whenever He comes, He brings super abundance. In an instant they had almost 180 gallons of choice wine comparable to Château d'Yquem, the most sought after wine in the world, a wine which sells thirty-six thousand pounds a bottle.

Defining this wine is no easy task. The wine is a straw yellow, darkening to gold and amber as it ages. It seems to pour more slowly than other sweet wines and, when swirled in the glass, clings more luxuriantly on the sides. The "Yquem" bouquet has being compared to peaches, figs, orange blossom and honey; even fresh-mown hay. Its taste has evoked descriptions that find in its extraordinary bouquet vanilla, apricots, and half the fruit under the sun.

Imagine that this couple should end up with over 180 gallons of choice wine that was better than Château d'Yquem. Overnight they were rich; Christ had come in and blessed them. They would be able to sell that wine and start a new life.

Today if you dare to invite Jesus into you life there is no telling what He will do but I can guarantee you this; if you trust His Word and do whatever He tells you to do, then He will in turn do for you more than you ever asked or imagined according to His power that is at work within you. (Ephesians 3: 20) There is God's power stored up in you, that is waiting to be put into use. So why not call it forth and let it be used to the glory of God.

Car manufacturer

Let's take for instance a car manufacturer. He manufactures a car with different parts ready to make up that car. He has in his factory a store where he stores spare parts for the car. If any one buys a car from, say, Toyota, any part of that car can be replaced at any time if damaged. It will only cost you money.

Today I also want you to know something about God who the Bible says "formed man". God being the one who created us, has in His store in heaven all the parts of our body that may be missing and it is easy for Him to replace them without surgery - a new vagina, womb, Fallopian tubes, missing genes, chromosomes, or whatever it is you may be lacking. If you only believe, then any or all of these things can be given to you.

In Isaiah 48: 6-7, the Bible says, "from now on I will tell you of new things, of hidden things unknown to you; they are created now and not long ago." Note the words "created now." God will create whatever you need now; now is the right time for you. The Bible says "you have not heard of them before today."

I am sure that, before you read this book, you did not know you could, by the help of the Holy Spirit and in Jesus' name, have new parts to replace any missing part of your body. The Bible clearly says when God sends His spirit all these new body parts are created. (Psalms 104: 30)

The Bible says that even in the beginning the earth was without form and void (empty) and darkness was upon the face of the deep. The spirit of God moved upon the face of the waters.

"And God said, 'Let there be light,' and there was light." (Genesis 1: 2) When God said, "Let there be light," immediately there was light - why? - because the Holy Spirit who creates life was already moving over the face of the waters. The Bible says that, "the same spirit is living within you and me." (Romans 8: 11) All we need to do is to speak from our mouths with faith (trust) what God's Word says concerning our need; then the spirit within us will start to create all that we need.

His power is already at work within us. The car manufacture will charge money to replace a missing part of your car - God will demand trust (faith) from you, enough faith to believe that, no matter how long it takes, He is able to create whatever body parts you may be missing to help you conceive. Even when our Lord Jesus turned water into wine, those servants had faith and were obedient to His instructions. It looked stupid in the normal way of things for them to take ordinary water to the master of the feast; after all, they knew that's what it was since they had filled those water pots themselves with water. But they obeyed our Lord Jesus and experienced a miracle that day.

Move out in faith

Many of you reading this book and desiring a creative miracle are going to have to move out of the normal zone to the supernatural zone, and believe, even when all around you scream, "stupid, impossible; it is not right; it can't be done." You will have to say, *"Yes, with God all things are possible."*

The next statement these servants heard was that the water was now choice wine; those words came from the lips of the master of the feast.

Faith and obedience

Faith and obedience will open any door for you. We read in the Bible of the women "who received back their dead, raised to life again." (Hebrews 11: 35) "Their dead" could mean many things. Here we will take the words to mean the missing vagina, womb, ovaries, Fallopian tubes, genes, chromosomes etc. The Bible goes on to say that these women's weakness were turned into strength. (Hebrews 11: 34)

The weakness you may be facing today may become your greatest strength - God will not only bless you but you can become a witness to many people who face the same situation if you dare to believe in God for what is impossible. You will bless many with your faith. If you are reading this book, then everything you read here is written through faith, because I dared to believe God - that what He told me to do He would bring to pass. I put all my hope and trust in Him and today this book has been written against all the odds.

God put a seed in you, the seed is there; don't let any lack stop you from having that child. You can hook up to God and become a victor. My pastor says: "a tea bag will not release its flavour till it's gone through hot water." You have gone through hot water, with God you can now release your flavour in Jesus' name, Why not? The master of the feast tasted the water that was turned into wine and said these words to the bridegroom: "Everyone brings out the choice wine first and then the cheaper wine, when the guests have had too much to drink, but you have saved the best till now." What a mighty God we serve! He has saved the best for you and the parts needed will be created immediately for the baby to come in Jesus' name.

Jesus came into that marriage that day, and blessed that couple, and saved them from embarrassment, He is able to do the same for you. He loves you and it matters to Him when your joy is not complete.

This is God's promise to you today :-

> No longer will you be ashamed, no longer will your face grow pale. When you see among you, your children, the work of my hands, then you will acknowledge the holiness of the holy one of Jacob and you will stand in awe of the God of Israel. (Isaiah 29: 22-23)

God not only promises you a child but children. He says you will end up standing in awe of Him.

Moves of faith

This is what was done in faith in this situation to bring about a miracle.

- The Lord was invited to this marriage.
- When a problem arose, He was the first person to be informed.
- When He gave an instruction it was obeyed. For the servants to fetch that water to the master of the feast required great faith because they did not know that water had turned into choice wine.
- This one act of obedience lead to a great blessing even though to the ordinary person it looked stupid.

Points of action

- Acknowledge God and Jesus as your Lord and Saviour.
- Invite Him into your home.
- Tell Him all your need in faith. If you need a creative miracle ask in faith for the Lord to create whatever organ you need.

- Tell Him to prove himself to you as He did for the Cana couple
- Tell Him to bless you with children as He promised in Psalms 127: 3
- Believe that He has done it.

- Start praising Him until there is full manifestation of all your blessings and continue praising Him after that, for He is worthy to be praised

Now make your confession

Father, I give you praise and I thank you. I thank you father that all you created is good and perfect. I know that I am fearfully and wonderfully made by you. Father in the name of Jesus I want to thank you for recreating my (*Name relevant body part*) in the name of Jesus. Your Word promises me creative miracles and by faith I receive it and thank you for it. I receive this creative miracle Father in the same way you did for the Cana couple when you turned their water into wine to glorify your name in their life. I thank you for doing the same for me. Mighty God I belive that " ...Christ has already borne my pain on the cross and by His stripes I was healed." (Isaiah 53:6) From today I am totally made whole and I will continue to walk in praise and worship of your name Father, beacause you are faithful. I am also rejoicing beacause I know that soon the sound of the cry and the smiles and laughter of a baby will be heard in our home to the glory of your name. I love you Father and I thank you in Jesus name. Amen.

Chapter Four

Where A Woman Is Sterilised

A woman is said to be sterile when she is barren. It is a state of permanent infertility, a permanent method of contraception in which the Fallopian tubes are sealed or cut to prevent a male's sperm from reaching the ovaries. Sterilisation is a common method of contraception.

Women who have completed their family or who plan not to have children may choose to be sterilised. Others, may choose to be sterilised due to danger to the health of the mother or high risk of children being born with hereditary disease.

The procedure of sterilisation involves blocking the Fallopian tubes by these methods: cutting, constriction or clipping or cautery. Any of these methods will stop the sperm reaching the ovaries, creating a state of permanent infertility.

Methods of sterilisation

Cutting

A small loop of the Fallopian tube may be drawn up, secured by a tight ligature, and then cut off.

Constriction

The loop is constricted by a tight band. Reversal is possible with this technique.

Clipping

A plastic or a metal clip may be applied to obstruct egg passage.

Cautery

Electro-coagulation (diathermy) can be used to burn through and thus seal the Fallopian tube.

A woman who might have been sterilised may, after remarriage, decide to have more children with her new partner. In some cases micro-surgical technique may succeed in restoring fertility in a woman who has been sterilised. In some cases it becomes impossible to reverse.

What the Bible says - Judges 13

Under the clear leadership of the Holy Spirit we go straight into the Bible. Today I invite you to take a journey with me in the Bible to the book of Judges. Our visit is to a man of Zorah, named Manoah; he was from the clan of the Danites, and had a wife who was sterile and remained childless. The angel of the Lord appeared to her and said, "You are sterile and childless but you are going to conceive and have a son. (Judges 13: 2-3) Here is an angel of the Lord telling this sterile lady that she is going to have a baby. We don't know the exact reason why she was sterile but one thing is clear - God was going to grant her a conception.

What did she do? She quickly went to her husband and told Him, "A man of God came to me, he looked like an angel of God, very awesome. I didn't ask him where he came from, and he didn't tell me his name but he said to me, you will conceive and give birth to a son"(Judges 13: 6).

What did she do? She did not start telling the man of God or the angel, "Oh, but my doctor said I can't have children; oh, but they said my health will be at risk if I get pregnant; oh, but my doctor said my children will have hereditary diseases if I get pregnant." That's how some people argue themselves out of their miracle. Today, please note carefully what this couple did because God asked me to write this book and told me exactly what to write. I believe every sterile woman who says yes to God, no matter what the best specialist in the world may have told her, will have healthy children without hereditary disease or any risk to her health, in Jesus' name.

Please note carefully what this wonderful woman did next. She received her message - her blessing - right away. She treasured it in her heart and went on to share her good news with her husband. She watched her words carefully; she did not start saying to her husband: "Darling, God must be joking. I have no womb, no Fallopian tube; how is this possible?" She did not negate the Word of God by saying negative things. Note again what that wonderful man did, "Then Manoah prayed to the Lord, 'O Lord, I beg you, let the man of God you sent to us come again to teach us how to bring up our boy who is to be born.' God heard Manoah's prayer and God sent the angel again to the woman while she was in the field but her husband was not with her."

Please, husbands, note something here; the man prayed, the angel came again a second time to the woman. Why? - because she was the one who needed faith more, to help her overcome her own limitations. Please, husbands, if your wife tells you her experience with God or what God told her, don't say to her, "Oh, if God is serious let him come and tell me, I am the head of this house." Don't use pride to rob your home of God's best for your family.

I really love this man Manoah; he was a real man of God. This couple loved God, they are winners any day, anywhere. Not once did they doubt God's Word to them; the husband was standing with his wife, trusting her words to be true and because of this the angel of God came to her again and Manoah got up and followed his wife, and when he came to the man he said, "Are you the one who talked to my wife?" "I am," he said. Manoah did not say, "All right; tell me once more." He only said these words to the angel of God: "When your words are fulfilled, what is to be the rule for the boy's life and work?"

In faith this couple took the promise of God and received that baby the same day. They never questioned God's Word, this couple totally depended and trusted God. They knew the God Who could offer more than enough, For the bible says:

Nothing is impossible with God. (Luke 1: 37)

And my God will meet all your needs according to his glorious riches in Christ Jesus. (Philippians 4: 19)

They knew the God who promised:

those who look to me are radiant, their faces are never covered with shame." (Psalms 34: 5)
They trusted the God

who settles the barren woman in her home as a mother of children. (Psalms 113: 9)

My advice to women who are sterile is this: put all your trust in God and his Word, Manoah's wife had put her trust in God. This woman had hooked up with God, she wanted that child, she prayed for that child. This woman knew how to attract angels when she cried, they came to

41

her; she loved God, God knew her voice and where she was because she was a praying woman, she was a fighting woman. She overcame sterility on her knees in prayer, not by running from place to place but on her knees. "Not long after this visit the woman conceived and gave birth to a son. They named him Samson."

Please don't say that was Bible days; many of us will be seeing more angels come, even in human form, to bring God's blessings into our lives. So please be careful how you treat the people who you meet - but don't go round looking for angels! God will manifest Himself to you anyway - He chooses but that is up to Him. But, for sure, you can have that child if you believe.

This is the action this couple took

- This couple was a praying couple. Prayer touches God, and when you touch God, He changes everything and brings you closer to Himself.

- This couple had total trust (faith) in God and God's Word.

- This couple were so smart they were not ready to negate God's promise by asking doubtful questions.

- This couple worked together in agreement for the Bible says that "whatever two shall agree on earth concerning anything, it shall be done for them." (Matthew 18: 19) This power is strongest in marriage.

- This couple's desire was to bring up their child in the way and in the fear of God. Why would God not bless such a couple?

Confession

Father I thank you that sterilisation is far from me; I am fertile and fruitful because your Word, which is active, has activated every part of my reproductive organs which were cut off when I was sterilised. I receive life in these organs because your Word is alive and effective. I thank you Father that you are rebuilding the old waste places of my life, I am like a green pine; and my fruitfulness comes from you. All that the canker worm

42

has eaten the Father is now restoring to me. Soon I will be announcing my good news in Jesus' name. Amen.

Question

1 What of the fear of my children being born with a hereditary disease?

One of the reason's given for sterilising a woman is the fear of the child being born with hereditary disease or fear of deformity. However, the Word of God is powerful and is able to override every situation.

I want to share with those women who are afraid of having a child that might be deformed or have Down's Syndrome etc, a testimony from the prayer I have written at the end of this chapter, this is to help you, encourage you and let you know that God's Word is true.

In 1995, the Lord was teaching me on the subject of fear of having handicapped children and I was writing everything He taught me. Just as I dropped my pen, my phone rang. It was my friend Ivell down the line, telling me that her friend who was pregnant had been told that the child in her womb would be born severely handicapped as revealed by the tests at the hospital.

The friend was confused as to what to do. I said to her, "I am just finishing a study on this issue. If I give you the prayer will your friend stand true to it. She said that yes, she would. So over the phone I dictated the whole prayer to her and she wrote it down for her friend.

Early in 1996 I received a phone call that the baby has been born normal, without any spot or blemish - a perfect baby boy to the glory of God.

What I want you to know is that the Word of God can and will always override every negative event that might happen in our life. The Word of God cannot only heal, it can create whatever part of the body you need or your baby needs to make it whole.

The Bible says, "the Word of God came to me saying, 'Before I formed you in the womb I knew you.'"- "your hand made me and formed me," Psalms 119:73- Whose hands? - God's hands. It is God who formed that child in your womb. He is the One Who gives form, shape and fashion to the human body. It is God who forms us, including the child you may desire to have and you are afraid of having. The Bible says that God has arranged the parts in the body, every one of them, just as he wanted them to be. (1 Corinthians 12: 18) What I am

43

trying to bring across to you is this: if your trust is in the Lord and you personally ask Him for a child, then you can also trust that He knows where to put each part to bring forth a perfect child. The Word of God says that we are fearfully and wonderfully made. (Psalms 139: 14) The Bible says every good and perfect gift comes from God (James 1: 17).

The Bible says you will not ask for bread and find God gives you a stone.

God is faithful. For those women who may be pregnant and are told, "sorry your baby is deformed," or this or that is wrong, please, I encourage you to trust and believe God. My friend's friend did and ended up with a beautiful child. Even for those women who are afraid of having handicapped children, I encourage you to take the prayer written down and apply it in your situation and God will help you in Jesus' name to stand and be victorious.

Prayers

For those women already pregnant

Father, in Jesus' name I worship you. I bless you and give you praise. Father, I come to you in Jesus' name and through the blood of Jesus Christ to ask you to protect and guide the baby in my womb. Thank you Father, that every good and perfect gift comes from you. You, yourself said all that you create or created is good (Genesis 1: 25). I thank you, Father, that this baby already formed is your workmanship according to Ephesians 2: 10. Father, all your works are beautiful and magnificent to behold. They are wonderfully finished. All your works are perfect, for every good and perfect gift comes from you (James 1: 17). I thank you for a perfect baby in Jesus' name. I condemn every tongue that has risen against me and my baby, in accordance with Isaiah 54: 17. I cover the baby in my womb with the precious blood of Jesus. Father, this prayer saved one baby and it will save mine in Jesus' name. Amen. This prayer can be said as often as you can - daily until there is full manifestation of all you want.

Prayer for women not yet pregnant

Father, I come to you in the name of Jesus Christ. I thank you and give you praise. Father I desire to conceive and have a baby but the doctors are saying my child will be at risk of (inherited disease). Father because I belong to you and to Jesus Christ, I am going ahead to have the baby.

You are my Father and you do not have any inherited disease in your body. So my children will only inherit life and good health which is what is in you. I have the divine nature of God in me.

Father, I condemn every evil report that has been written about me and I declare that I am going to go ahead and have a healthy baby in the name of Jesus. I cover my womb and the coming baby in the blood of Jesus. Amen.

What of the threat to my health?

Prayer

Father, in the name of Jesus Christ, I bless you and worship you. Father, thank you for your love and mercy to me. Father, you created me as a woman to bring forth children into the world.

Father, in Jesus' name, hear that I have been told by doctors that a pregnancy endangers my life. Father, your promise to me is that I will be like a fruitful vine within my husband's house. A fruitful vine is full of grapes. It is never dry. (Psalms 128: 3) Your Word says you will grant me abundant prosperity - in the fruit of my womb. (Deuteronomy 28: 11)

Your promise to me is total victory in all areas of life because the blood of Jesus was shed for me. Isaiah 53: 5 says "Christ was pierced for my transgressions, he was crushed for my iniquities, the punishment that brought us peace was upon him, and by his wounds we are healed. " Father, I stand firm by your promises and declare that I will go on and have this baby. Father, I will not worry about medical reports, I am going to stand by the finished work Christ has done for me. You, Lord, told me to cast my cares upon you. I cast all my cares upon you and I leave them there. Thank you for total victory, in Jesus' name. Amen.

This prayer is to be said as many times as you can every day until there is full manifestation of all you desire.

Chapter Five

Damage That Can Occur To The Reproductive Organs

Defects of the womb

Defects of the womb(uterus) are some of the main causes of infertility. The uterus is situated in the pelvic cavity. This is where, after its long journey through the Fallopian tube, the fertilised egg finally embeds and starts to develop from an embryo into a baby for about forty weeks.

The lower part of the uterus opens into the vagina at the neck of the cervix, the upper part of the uterus opens into the Fallopian tube. The uterus is where the foetus grows and any defect can prevent the implantation of the embryo.

Problems that affect the womb

There are two types of growths that occur in the womb. These growths can either be benign or malignant.

We now look at them individually.

Benign growths - means the growth that does not spread.

Fibroid

This is a benign growth of the uterus. This growth may be as small as a pea or can grow up to the size of a grapefruit. There could be one or more. fibroids consist of smooth muscles, bundles and connective tissue that keeps growing slowly within the uterine wall. It attaches itself to a stalk and keeps growing, sometimes protruding from the uterus walls into the uterine cavity causing it to become distorted. Most fibroids may not produce symptoms while some may cause pains such as backache or even stomach pain; some may lead to prolonged bleeding during menstruation, and severe bleeding can lead to anaemia. Some large fibroids can exert pressure on the bladder, causing discomfort or frequent passing of urine, or constrict the bowel. Fibroids that distort the uterine cavity may lead to miscarriage or infertility. Medically the cause of fibroids is not known. In serious cases fibroids have lead to hysterectomy.

Growths affecting the cervix

What is the cervix?

The cervix is a small cylindrical organ in the body of the woman. It comprises the lower part and the neck of the womb. The cervix separates the body and the cavity of the uterus from the vagina. Running through the cervix is the canal through which the sperm pass from the vagina into the uterus and through which blood passes during menstruation. The cervical canal forms part of the birth canal during childbirth.

Cancer of the cervix

Cancer of the cervix (the neck of the womb) is one of the most common cancers affecting women world-wide. If untreated it may spread to most of the organs in the pelvis. The chance of medical cure depends very much on what stage the cancer has reached when first diagnosed.

There are two types of cervical cancer:

Squamous type

This is very common and is almost certainly the result of some process that occurs during sexual intercourse, possibly involving an infectious organism acquired from the male partner. A woman in a sexual relationship with a man who has genital warts has about a one-in-three risk of developing a pre-cancerous condition of the cervix.

Smoking: smokers are at higher risk than non-smokers, possibly because smoking impairs the body's immune system's natural defence against infection and so allows entry and proliferation of a causative virus. Another alternative explanation is that the chemical carcinogen in cigarettes is absorbed into the blood stream and excreted into the cervical secretions.

Additional evidence in favour of this theory is the observation that the incidence of cervical cancer is affected by the smoking habits of women's male partners. The sexual behaviour of the woman and her male partners strongly influence her chances of developing the disease.

Adenocarcinoma

This is a much rarer type of cervical cancer which affect both sexually active woman and those who have never had intercourse before. The pre-cancerous stages cause no symptoms whatever. The malignant stages are also initially few. Eventually, a woman will notice vaginal bleeding or a blood-stained discharge at unexpected times - between periods, after intercourse or after the menopause.

If left untreated, the cancer spreads from the cervical surface into the deeper parts of the cervix and then out into the pelvic tissue, causing pain. Eventually the cancer spreads to the bladder, rectum, and surrounding pelvic tissue.

Polyp

This a form of growth on the cervix. This growth projects, usually on a stalk from the lining of the cervix. Some are benign and some are likely to become malignant, leading to cancer.

Benign tumours affecting placental tissue

Hydatidiform mole

This tumour develops from placental tissue in early pregnancy where the embryo did not develop normally. It normally looks like a cluster of small grapes. The cause of this is degeneration of the chronic villi, these are minute finger-like projections in the placenta. If this tumour is not treated earlier it could lead to a malignant tumour invading the wall of the womb.

Ovarian cyst

The ovary is situated on either side of the womb below the opening of the Fallopian tube. The ovary has numerous cavities called follicles where eggs develop. The ovaries also produce the female sex hormones oestrogen and progesterone and a small amount of the male sex hormone, testosterone. An ovarian cyst is an abnormal fluid-filled swelling in one of the ovaries.

Dermoid Cysts

These cysts normally have cell structures that look similar to that of the skin, containing hair, sweat glands and sebaceous glands. The cysts may even contain fragments of cartilage, bone and even teeth. These account for about ten percent of ovarian tumours.

Follicular Cyst

In this case the egg-producing follicle of the ovary enlarges and fills up with fluid. In other cases the cyst may grow in the corpus luteum, a yellow mass of tissue that forms from the follicle after ovulation. These benign growths can occur at any age.

Malignant Growths

Malignant growths are growths that are cancerous and spread around the affected areas.

Choriocarcinoma tumour

This is a rare malignant tumour that develops from the placenta in the uterus. It is derived from cells in the placental attachment of the fertilised ovum to the wall of the uterus. This usually arises as a result of a benign tumour turning into a malignant one. This often results after an abortion because it is very rare after a normal pregnancy.

However, if untreated, it invades and starts to destroy the walls of the uterus. It may even spread to the vagina and vulva. This tumour, if not treated early, could spread to affect the lungs, liver, brain and bones.

Cancer of the uterus -This is a malignant growth in the tissue of the uterus. This normally affects both the cervix and endometrium (uterus lining). Cancer of the endometrium is common in women who have excess oestrogen hormones in their system or where the progesterone level is low. Failure to ovulate could also be a cause.

Ovarian cancer - This is a malignant growth in the ovary. This growth may take the form of a growth in the ovary or may arise as a secondary growth that spreads to the ovary from some other part of the body, because of the spreading nature of this growth. It could lead to a hysterectomy (removal of the ovaries, womb, uterus etc.) in some cases.

I may not have written down the name of the growth you may be having to face but don't worry about it. Just take the Word of God and apply it to any growth. It is the same principle and it will work on all growths in Jesus' name. God bless you.

What the Bible says about these growths

The first thing I want you to know is this; your womb belongs to God. The Bible says that the first offspring of every womb belongs to God (Exodus 34: 19). The Word of God says that the fruit of your womb is blessed (Deuteronomy 28: 4).

If God says the fruit of your womb is blessed, what is a growth doing in your womb? Can you offer these growths to God? The answer is no. Because you cannot offer these growths to God, these growths must give way for a baby in Jesus' name.

Taking a journey through the pages of the Bible, under the leadership of the Holy Spirit we now see what God has to say about these growths. We normally class these growths into benign and malignant, meaning that the benign growths are less difficult to treat than the malignant ones which are classed as the cancerous ones. That's OK for man but in the presence of Almighty God, growths, whether benign or malignant, become the same before God. God does not see these growths the way you and I see them. So what I have written here is applicable to both benign and malignant growths and I want you to get this clear spiritually. The Bible says that God's arms are not too short to rescue you; neither does He lack the strength to rescue you. For by a mere rebuke God dries up the sea, turning rivers into a desert (Isaiah 50: 2). If God is able to turn a whole river into dry land by one word, what hope is there for any growth to remain in your womb, after the Word of God is spoken to it? I can boldly tell you now, no growth can withstand the power of God's Word in the name of Jesus Christ.

The thing about some of these growths is that they attach themselves to a stalk and project themselves and keep growing like stems on a plant but this is what God has promised to do to these growths. He says, "if there were briers (a plant with a woody, thorny or prickly stem) and thorns bearing sharp pickles of thorn) confronting me I would march against them in battle; I would set them all on fire" (Isaiah 27: 3-4) - That's exactly the description that best fits these growths and exactly

50

what God plans to do to them, for our God is a consuming fire. (Deuteronomy 4: 24)

The effect of the consuming fire depends on our relationship with Him. The fire will destroy all stubble and all dross, but it purifies and heals all those who are in the right relationship with Him. The Bible says "the sun of righteousness shall arise with healing in his wings." Many people who have received divine healing have described a feeling of heat or burning in their body as the fire of God consumes every growth or disease that has tried to plant and attach itself in their womb or bodies.

I want to tell you what the Bible says in Psalm 97: 5 "that every mountain melts like wax before the Lord of all the earth." Every difficult or impossible situation is classed in the Bible as a mountain. Here the Bible is telling us that the growths will melt like wax at the name of the Lord - that the sun of righteousness arises with healing in its wings. The sun will usually rise with scorching heat and light radiating from it. So also God's son, Jesus Christ, arises with heat and righteousness (a sense of justice) to do that which is right by destroying all growths attached to the wombs of his daughters.

The Bible says, "they swarmed around me like bees (these growths) but they died out as quickly as burning thorns; in the name of the Lord (Psalms 118: 12). God promises us that these benign and malignant growths that look so tough and difficult to treat will melt like wax when the Word is spoken to them. He promises that these growths that swarm around like bees attacking will quickly die down as burning thorns when the Word is spoken to it. The Bible says "the Lord is in His holy temple; He observes the sons of men, his eyes examine them, on the wicked (cancer) he will rain fiery coals and burning sulphur (Psalm 11:4-6).

I want to encourage you not to be afraid of growths. Speak the Word of God to them. I want you to hold on to this biblical promise: "See the name of the Lord comes from afar, with burning anger and dense clouds of smoke; his lips are full of wrath, and his tongue is a consuming fire (Isaiah 30: 27). When your God speaks, fire comes out of his mouth; consuming fire is what comes out, so speak the Word of God from your lips and let the wrath of God consume growths from your body in the name of Jesus.

From these scriptures we see God's Word and know therefore what is to be done to these growths. God's Word promise that those growths will die out, "melt like wax", at the name of the Lord.

Now we will apply these Bible promises to these growths with the power of our words, lining them up with God's Word. Now say your-

Prayer

Father, I come before you in the name of Jesus Christ through the blood He shed on the Cross for me. I thank you for your grace and mercy. I bless you for your goodness. I thank you that in Christ I am blessed and fruitful. Father, hear, the doctors have diagnosed growths in my womb, but by your Word, which the Bible says is sharp, I cut off all these growths that try to grow in my womb. These growths have swarmed around my womb like bees, but today I command them to die down as quickly as burning thorns through the name of Jesus Christ. I declare that every growth has been sharply cut off from my womb by your Word and melted like wax according to your Word. I cover my womb in the blood of Jesus.

Father, I thank you because I was cast down and was about to lose my womb but you have healed me. You, O! Lord! are my strength and my song. Father, I thank you and I bless you. In Jesus' name.

Your daily confession

▰ My womb is blessed and fruitful. The fruit of my womb is blessed, where there was only growth before, now there is life, because God's Word has sharply cut off every growth and the breadth of His mouth has melted it like wax. My womb is ready to receive life because it is blessed by Almighty God.

▰ The root of cancer (Name growth) is cursed. This growth has become like the seed which fell on rocky places, where it did not have much soil......the Son of God has shone His light upon it and destroyed it with His powerful Word. It is scorched and withered and will never find root again in my womb in Jesus name. Amen.(Mark 4:5-6)

▰ The Judgement of God is come upon this cancer, with the words of my mouth anointed by the Holy Spirit I declare that you are withered and melted like wax. Gods judgement has flashed like lightening upon you. You will never regrow or come near my womb or my body in Jesus mighty Name - Amen (Hosea 6:5).

When you say your confession sit in a comfortable place. As you say the word actually visualise the word of God melting that growth from your womb. The Word of God works. God bless you.

Chapter Six

Damage To The Fallopian Tubes

The Fallopian tube

This is the tube situated in the pelvis with each tube extending from an ovary to the upper part of the uterus. The Fallopian tube transports both egg and sperm and is where fertilisation takes place. The fertilised egg becomes an embryo and then it travels along the Fallopian tube into the uterus. Below are some of the problems likely to affect the Fallopian tubes.

Ectopic pregnancy

Any blockage to the Fallopian tube can cause servere problems, particually one caused by an ectopic pregnancy. This is where the egg that is fertilised starts to grow in the tube instead of travelling through to the womb. This could lead to rupture or damage to the tubes. An ectopic pregnancy can, on occasions, be an indication that the tubes are not functioning properly in the first place.

Inflammation or Swelling

Any inflammation or swelling at the wall of the tubes or scar tissue could lead to a blockage of the Fallopian tube. If one tube is blocked the other could also be blocked. In some cases the lining of the tube could be damaged, in such a cases the egg and sperm cannot meet each other, because the tiny hair-like projection that waft eggs and sperm together may be damaged.

Bacteria Infection

E coli bacteria and some type of streptococci bacteria can lead to infection that could block the Fallopian tube. Those most likely to be affected are those who live promiscuous lifestyles because sexually transmitted disease like chlamydia and gonorrhoea lead to inflammation and tubal blockage and if not treated can lead to infertility. Miscarrage and abortion can also lead to infection occurring in a woman's womb which could cause tube blockage. Any surgery in the region of a woman's pelvis such as for a ruptured appendicitis could years later lead to tubal block or damage making it impossible for eggs to pass through.

Endometriosis

This condition is where the cells that normally line a woman's womb spread to other parts of her body. They may start growing in her Fallopian tubes, or around her ovaries or bladder. In most cases these cell patches may prevent eggs entering the Fallopian tubes or block them by preventing a growing embryo from passing into the womb. These cells may also release chemicals into the Fallopian tube.

Adenomyosis

This is where the lining of the womb becomes abnormally thick, leading to painful periods and pain during sexual intercourse. This will normally affect small patches of the womb but if large areas are involved and if the thickening is at the point where the Fallopian tubes enters the womb, this can lead to blockage of the tubes.

I have listed above the problems that affect the Fallopian tubes or even those which affect the womb and lead to blockage of the tubes.

What the Bible says

By the leadership of the Holy Spirit, we now go into the Word of God to see what God has to say in Jesus' name about blocked Fallopian tube.

"He has walled me in so that I cannot escape; he has barred my way with blocks of stone; he has made my path crooked." (Lamentations 3:7-8) This description from the Bible best describes the blockage of the Fallopian tubes. What is a tube? The dictionary describes a tube as a slender channel that can be within a human body. The Fallopian tube is a long channel within the body of a woman; it is like a long road through which sperm travels into the womb but when it is barred or blocked due to one thing or the other, it becomes impossible for the sperm to pass through.

The sperm is walled in and cannot escape. Its passage is barred by (scar tissue), making it impossible for fertilisation to take place, but the Bible says: "…with the help of the Lord you can scale a wall." (Psalms 18: 29) So the wall of stone built around your tubes can be commanded to melt like wax at the name of the Lord. (Psalms 97: 5) You can become a victor instead of a victim in Jesus' name. The problem you

54

are facing today could become your testimony to the glory of God.

The Bible says this about blocked Fallopian tubes; because of the Lord's great compassion we are not defeated by blocked Fallopian tubes and infertility, "for His compassion never fails, and is renewed every morning; great is His faithfulness." (Lamentations 3: 22-23) The Father is truly faithful and nobody who put their trust in Him will ever be put to shame.

Hannah's blocked Fallopian tubes

The best illustration of blocked Fallopian tubes in the Bible is Hannah. The Bible records in 1 Samuel 1: 6: "…that the Lord had closed her womb." This essentially involved the closure of the Fallopian tubes. This is because the Fallopian tube is like a door or passage which can be closed or blocked.

Hannah's tubes were closed but she kept on praying to the Lord. One day the pastor of the church where she was praying came in and saw how desperately she was praying; he thought she was drunk but she said to him. "No I am not drunk, I am only praying my heart out to the Lord."

The pastor of that church blessed her and said: "Go in peace; may the Lord grant you what you asked him." The Bible says, "the Lord remembered Hannah in the course of time and she conceived and gave birth to a son. (I Samuel 1: 19-20)

Many women today face Fallopian tube problems but please get this clear in your spirit, no matter the cause of the tubal blockage, at the name of Jesus it will have to open. In Lamentations 3: 7-9, it says "he has walled me in so that I cannot escape. He has barred my way with blocks of stone," which could be scar tissue or whatever is causing blockage of your tubes. "He has made my way crooked," which could be a rupture to the tube due to infection or whatever, and this prevents sperm and egg from meeting.

You might have noticed that in the Bible it never told us the method God used to close Hannah's womb but her Fallopian tubes were closed. But the "Lord determined to tear down the wall around the daughter of Zion," (that is you) in Jesus' name. (Lamentations 2: 8) The Lord has already determined to tear down the wall that is built around your Fallopian tubes. Hannah would not give up; she kept praying, she kept trusting God and because of her prayer God opened her womb, and He removed whatever was blocking her tubes and blessed her with a son. If you will trust God and hold on to Him He will do the same for you, for our God is no respecter of persons.

Joshua 6

The second story I want us to look at is in Joshua 6. You may be wondering what this story has got to do with blocked Fallopian tubes but through the guidance of the Holy Spirit, we will see that the two problems are the same.

The formidable wall of Jericho

Now Jericho was tightly shut up because of the Israelites. No one went in, no one went out. There on the plains of Jericho, Joshua and the children of Israel faced the formidable barrier of the wall of Jericho, which in the natural way of things was impossible to penetrate.

Now your Fallopian tube is blocked or tightly shut up due to one problem or the other, sperms being unable to go through the tube neither can any egg be fertilised. Why? This is because the devil is afraid of the child you will give birth to. The reason is that the child will destroy his kingdom.

The Fallopian tubes are so delicate and even an attempt to unblock them, tends in most cases to create more problems.

Then the Lord said to Joshua, "See, I have delivered Jericho into your hands, along with its fighting men."

Although, you face an enemy who is infertility due to blocked Fallopian tubes, this is what God says to you: "Because you love me says the Lord, I will rescue you (from blocked Fallopian tubes). I will protect you, for you acknowledge my name. I will be with you in trouble, I will deliver you from Fallopian tube blockage and honour you." (Psalm 91: 14-15) Please listen carefully to what God told Joshua to do next and if you apply the same principles it will bring you victory in Jesus' name.

"Do this for six days; make seven priests carry trumpets of ram's horn in front of the ark." What was the purpose of these trumpets? A trumpet is an instrument of praise; even though they were ordered not to blow them, but march around carrying them for six days it was still an instrument of praise. The trumpet represented a symbol of praise to God, the Bible actually says that God inhabits the praise of His people.

When we praise Him, we prepare the way for His blessing to rest upon us.

God loves to hear us praise Him. When we start to praise Him, He comes down to live in our praise and when He comes, He comes with blessings, including babies. So fly up, upon the wings of praise. So Joshua called the priest and said to them, "Take up the ark of the covenant of the Lord and make seven priests carry trumpets in front of it. March around the city, with the armed guard going ahead of the ark." (Joshua 6: 6) When you start praising God for His love and mercy and His goodness, God will Himself manifest himself to you. "On the seventh day, they got up at daybreak and marched around the city seven times in the same manner. Except that on that day they circled the city seven times."

The seventh time around, when the trumpets sounded, the people gave a loud shout; the wall collapsed so every man charged straight in and they took the city. (Joshua 6: 15-20) I have since noticed something about God that still amazes me even now. The victories God gives are sure and when they come you will always know they are through God. What kind of war plan is this? Circle round a fortified city for seven days carrying trumpets and then on the seventh day shout and the wall will come down? No board meetings, no guns, no emergency military training; just praise. No wonder God said to us: "I will contend with those who contend with you. I will give safety to your children and I will ease them." (Isaiah 49: 25)

What does contend mean? It means to strive in a contest or against difficulties; to strive in debate, argue, maintain, assert. God has promised us that He himself will contest for us against difficulties. He will fight for us, He will stand for us. He has promised us that, "No weapon formed against us will prosper (Isaiah 54: 17) Why? - because He is the one fighting for us. The battle belongs to the Lord.

He says, "I will turn all the mountains into roads." (Isaiah 49: 11) which means all that scar tissue blocking the road, (Fallopian tubes) will melt like wax before the Lord, at the name of Jesus Christ. He said, "I am the way;" God will lead those sperm on the right way through your Fallopian tubes if you praise Him and call upon His name because He alone is the way.

Blocked or damaged Fallopian tubes will become afraid when they hear the praises of God rising within your belly everyday. Have you ever wondered why God commanded the barren woman to sing in Isaiah 54: 1?

57

"Sing, o barren woman, you who never bore a child; burst into song, shout for joy, you who were never in labour because more are the children of the desolate woman." You then may say, "Oh Lord, I don't feel much like singing. I have gone through so much pain what is there to sing about in this situation?"

God then replies to you and explains why He has commanded you to sing.

"Enlarge the place of your tent, stretch your tent curtains wide; do not hold back:; lenghten your cords, strengthen your stakes, for you will spread out (with children) to the right and to the left." (Isaiah 54: 2-3)

Not only will He bless you with one child but with as many children as you want. As you continue to sing, the promise gets better - "your descendants will dispossess nations and settle in their desolate cities." (Isaiah 54: 3)

Not only this but as you continue to praise, these children will have their own children who in turn will have their own children, until your descendants become so great.

As the praise of God rises in your belly, blockages start to melt away and the tubes are cleared to receive life in Jesus' name.

That is exactly what God did to the wall of Jericho; as the children of God praised Him each day the wall was gradually weakened from its foundation until it finally collapsed on the seventh day, as a result of the use of the weapons of praise and worship. There is power in praise, there is victory in praise; there is no wall that can stand the power of praise. Blocked Fallopian tubes will open up as you start to praise God.

By any natural law what God had directed them to do seemed foolish. There was absolutely no possibility that by marching around the city and shouting that the wall would crumble and fall. But God had a two-fold purpose in giving them this strategy.

1 He wanted them to know, beyond any doubt - in this very first battle, in taking possession of the city - that He was with them and it was He who would give them victory.
2 He wanted to teach them not to rely upon their own strength, but to look to Him and trust Him to fulfil His promise and make them victorious over all their enemies.

I want to link both Bible accounts to encourage you and let you know our God is able. In the first account we saw Hannah, a woman whose Fallopian tubes were blocked for many years. She did not stop praying and praising God and finally God blessed her with a son - not only one son but Hannah went on to have three more sons and two daughters (I Samuel 2: 21) making her a proud mother of six.

In the second account we see the children of God face the formidable barrier of the wall of Jericho. In any natural way the wall was beyond them. There was nothing they could have done to bring down that wall and take the city. But God Himself fought for them. In the midst of their obeying His instructions, that wall came down by the power of God. Today you may face the wall of blocked Fallopian tubes, you may have done all you know how to do without success. I just encourage you to praise God and just watch what He will do. The God who did it for Hannah and for the children of Israel will do it for you. Blocked Fallopian tubes are not a problem to God.

Today God is requiring the same of you. He wants you to look up to Him, rely on Him and trust Him to give you victory in all areas of life even when your problem is blocked Fallopian tubes.

Points for action

* Come to God by faith.
* Tell Him the *problem you face.*
* Tell Him what you desire for Him to do for you and believe you have received it
* Thank Him for it through faith
* Then start to praise Him - the more the praise, the quicker the victory. God bless you.

Take the confession written below and confess and praise God more often than you used to. Very soon you will be pregnant in Jesus' name.

Confession

Father I thank you for your grace and mercy. I come to you today in the name of Jesus Christ and I bless you. I thank you that in Christ I am blessed and fruitful. Your Word is powerful. It has performed surgery on my Fallopian tubes removing any blockage that exists; it has repaired all damage that existed. Every curse of the law is bound. My Fallopian tubes are open in the name of Jesus. I am free from every curse of infertility. My tubes can now transport life in Jesus' name. Thank you Father for glorifying your name in my life in Jesus' name. Amen.

Chapter Seven

The Ovaries

What are the ovaries?

The ovaries are a pair of almond-shaped glands situated on both sides of the womb below the Fallopian tube opening. The ovaries consist of numerous egg cells and egg-producing follicles. The ovaries do not only produce eggs but also the female hormones, oestrogen and progesterone.

Problems that affect the ovaries

• Damage due to an accident or infection. Sometimes a woman's ovaries may be present but contain eggs that have become severely damaged through accident or infection.

• Medically, after a long period of treatment, it may become apparent that nothing is going to stimulate an egg to develop.

Premature menopause

This is where a woman seems to run out of or stop releasing eggs as early as their mid-twenties. It appears that their ovaries run out of eggs. Menstruation stops and female hormone levels fall, leading to premature menopause. Without treatment these women start to succumb to many diseases that we associate with old age.

Hormone

A woman's hormone level is always changing in a well-ordained pattern that is vital for egg development, release and subsequent implantation of a fertilised embryo. If any of the three main source of hormones, the pituitary gland, the thyroid gland or the hypothalamus is not operating properly, this could lead to problems. Over-production of hormones is equally capable of upsetting the process.

(PCOD) Polycystic Ovary Syndrome

This is where the ovaries become packed full of follicular cysts that can grow quite large and impede the development of eggs. Women who experience this problem find that when they start their period it is normal but as time goes on it becomes scanty or absent. This is as a result of the body producing excess testosterone (male sex hormones) which women normally produce but only in small amounts. Too much of this hormone could put a woman's system off-balance leading to over-stimulation of the ovaries, causing the eggs not to mature properly and not to be released. This leads to cessation of menstruation and infertility.

Where a woman's body produces anti-bodies that destroy the sperm

This is where the woman's cervical mucus produces anti-bodies that are hostile to the sperm and immobilise them or destroy them.

I notice a pattern of problems running through the hormones problems listed above. All these problems affect either the production of the eggs or lead to other major problems. Before I go further, I would like us to understand what the eggs a woman makes are. This will help us to understand better as we go into the Bible.

The Ovum

About one month after a female embryo is fertilised and starts to develop, a group of cells now specialise and become her ovaries. These incompletely formed ovaries will move into position within the embryo and start to grow. By the time the girl is born the ovaries will contain a few million eggs; by the time of birth, the number of eggs will already have started to reduce.

After a girl's birth her ovaries produce no new egg cells. The surviving cells are immature and they need to wait patiently until the girl reaches puberty. At puberty only half a million or less will remain of which four or five hundred may be released; out of this only a few will be fertilised by the sperm and make babies.

So we see that a woman's eggs are her seed. It is what she has to plant to bring life. Without it she will never be able to give life.

All the problems that we describe are attacks on the seed of the woman.

Under the guidance of the Holy Spirit we will now go into the Word of God to see what God has to say about these ovulation problems. In all these ovulating problems the key issue is that life is wasting away and all that remains is death. Where a woman's eggs run out, or her ovaries fail to make eggs or the hormone balance of her body is not regulating her hormonal system any more, all she faces is disappointment and sorrow.

A woman said this about her ovulatory problems: "I faced a bereavement." What is bereavement? It is loss through death.

Going through the Bible I would like to introduce you to my Lord and Saviour Jesus Christ and in knowing Him you will know that He alone is the sustainer of life that is ebbing or wasting away. The sign we will be looking at was given by the Lord to the dying or those sorrowing because death was near, either for a loved one, or even for you who face ovulatory problems.

We go straight into the book of John to see what Jesus did for a person who faced the same problem you face and through this problem God brought great joy and victory to that home.

Jesus the sustainer of life

Once more he (Jesus) visited Cana in Galilee, where he had turned water into wine. And there was a certain royal official whose son lay sick at Capernaum. When this man heard that Jesus had arrived in Galilee from Judah, he went to him and begged him to come and heal his son who was close to death. "Unless you people see miraculous signs and wonders," Jesus told him, "you will never believe." The royal official said, "Sir, come down before my child dies." Jesus replied, "You may go, your son will live." (John 4: 46-54)

The man took Jesus at His Word and departed. While he was still on the way, his servant met him with the news that his boy was alive. When he enquired as to the time his son got better, they said to him, "the fever left him yesterday at the seventh hour." Then the father realised that this was the exact time at which Jesus had said to him, "your son will live." So he and all his household believed. (John 4: 46-54)

First we see a man who faced the death of his only son. Quite a young boy for that matter. A deadly fever held this boy in its grip. Other help must have been sought by this father for his son but without success. If money could have done it, the boy would have been healed already because it is quite clear this man was rich, but all attempts from the human side had failed. Thus the father came to our Lord and cried to Him saying, "Come and heal my son, who is close to death."

For women who have PCOD, or premature menopause, or damage to the ovaries that stop their eggs from being released, you know that this is an attack on the seed in you. This seed is the life of the children you desire to have and yet without this seed you can never be a fully biological mother.

This father faced a hopeless situation which from the human standpoint looked totally impossible; yet what can man do without God. For the woman who face the problems mentioned above you know some of these cases are beyond any medical help. No doctor or drugs can help you. When we look at the symptoms of some of these problems we see impossibilities - man's impossibilities. No doctor or drugs can help, It is a hopeless situation. No amount of money can buy any of these things for you; however, all of these illnesses can be healed by God.

Next, the father heard that Jesus had arrived in Galilee from Judea - he went to Him and begged Him to come and heal his son who was close to death. For the woman who faces the above problem, the life of your children are likewise wasting away. I want to introduce you to Jesus. The noble man heard that Jesus was in town, someone told him.

Jesus stands at the door of your heart and knocks

Today, I am also telling you that Jesus is not only in town, He is standing right at the door of your heart and is knocking, asking you to open up and invite Him to come in to your life and help you. He himself said, "Because I live, you will also live. On that day you will realise that I am in the Father, and you are in me and I am in you." (John 14: 19-20) When you invite Him, like the royal official did, and you say to Him, "Lord, heal me from premature menopause or help me - my eggs are not developing, the life source of my womanhood is ebbing away, my hope of being a mother is wasting away; only you can help. He will surely do it for you.

You don't need to say to Him, Lord please come, because He is already at the door of your heart, just ask. Ask in simple faith, [trust] and He will manifest himself to you. Say, "Lord come and dwell in my heart by faith."

Jesus then said to the royal official, "Unless you people see miraculous signs and wonders, you will not believe." Why did He make that statement? Here we see a father in need and judging from our Saviour's record we see that He is always ready to help the needy even when they do not ask for it. This statement was made as a stern reproof to this man and to all men and secondly as an encouragement to those men and to all men in the world.

The desire for signs condemned by our Lord

The desire for signs and wonders was in the spirit of the Jews in those days. The Jews required a sign. Our Lord mourns over the unspiritual state that demands marvellous manifestation before people will believe. Our generation has been caught in the same spirit - the desire to see signs and wonders before believing.

Our Lord often gave signs to help faith, but He goes on to say "Blessed are those who have not seen and yet believe." (John 20: 29) This statement was made by our Lord as a result of one of his disciples Thomas who was told that Jesus had risen from the dead. He said to them, "Unless I see the nail marks on his hands and put my finger where the nails were, and put my hands into his side, I will not believe it." A week later Jesus appeared to them again while Thomas was there. Then He said to Thomas. "Put your finger here, see my hands, reach out your hand and put them into my side, stop doubting and believe." Thomas said to Him, "My Lord and my God." Then Jesus said to him. "Because you have seen me, you have believed; blessed are those who have not seen, yet have believed." (John 20: 25-29)

Our Lord will give us signs to help our faith, but He would rather we believe Him even when there is no sign given. He would rather we take His Word for what it is, than build our faith on signs.

Ask And You Will Receive

For you who face the above-mentioned problems I want you to treasure in your heart this promise from God. Jesus said, "I tell you the truth, my father will give you whatever you ask in my name. Until now you have not asked for anything in my name. Ask and you will receive and your joy will be complete." (John 16: 23-24) A lot of times our Lord healed those who did not ask for it, but His perfect will for us is to ask. He loves to hear you ask Him, He loves to hear that we need Him, He loves to hear our voice, so ask Him for what you need. Let your hope be built on His words, His promise, rather than on signs and wonders. For He who believes even when He does not yet see is already blessed.

His faith grew

The more the noble man was in the presence of our Lord, the more he realised that His son's life depended upon the presence and actions of Jesus. He thought that by Jesus coming physically to his home, a cure would be effected. But today I want to encourage any woman who faces this problem to know that Jesus does not need to travel down from heaven to meet with you. Christ is not limited by either time or space, He is already with you through the Holy Spirit; no boundaries of life or time can hinder His working. Even if all your eggs are dead, Jesus is the resurrection and the life. For He said, "Just as the Father raises the dead and give them life, so the son gives life to whom he is pleased to give it." (John 5 :21) Jesus is pleased to give life to you if you will reach out in faith and receive, beacause no defeat or death exists in the presence of the Lord. There is hope for you through Christ Jesus. This man's faith grew as Jesus made clear to Him the defect in his faith, revealing to Him that true belief rests upon simple trust and obedience rather than excitement and feelings.

True spiritual understanding

When the noble man understood the spiritual reality of who Jesus was, he became convinced and this led him to put all his trust in the words of our Lord even though his presence could not be seen - because the Lord would not follow Him home.

The Test

Our Lord tested the inward sincerity of the man's faith and when He grew sincere instead of becoming angry, the blessing desired was granted abundantly, more than He had asked.

For any woman facing these problems, your inward sincerity will be tested. If you are sincere, God will meet you at the point of your need, but if all you want is to play games with the Lord, you may never know who Jesus is or receive the best He has for you. You can deceive human beings but you cannot deceive Him because He looks at the heart.

Perfected Faith - On his Word

When Jesus said to the nobleman, "No, I will not be coming to Capernaum with you but go, your son lives," the man did not become disappointed but his faith now rested upon the words of our Lord Jesus and he travelled home leisurely, for it was on the following day that he arrived home. He did not start running home in a hurry to see if his son was still alive but he took his time. His faith was intact, he had the peace of God in him after Jesus spoke to him. He knew all was well. He trusted Jesus.

For the women who face these problems, God's promise to you is that whatever you ask Him in the name of Jesus, He will do it for you. Will you, like the noble man, believe this promise and rely upon it, knowing that his words cannot fail? When our faith is perfected the essential request is granted.

Methods

God will always manifest Himself to us but we may not always get the answer the way we expected it; but we will always be answered if we believe. God will not allow us to reduce Him to a recipe - that is why no one can ever predict Christ's timing and way of answering prayers. His time is always the best and He is never late. This I have learnt myself over the few years of walking with the Lord. When you pray, leave the methods to Him, don't try to order Him around by telling Him what, when and how to do things, it doesn't work. He comes in time and harkens to us in His own time and way.

For the women facing these problems, if you have gone through fertility treatments, I know you have been told a lot about impossibilities. But today I want you to know that with God all things are possible. Don't try to figure out how and what God is going to do to help you. When you have prayed, go your way like the noble man did when Jesus told Him to; do not delay for if your trust is in Him and His Word, He will be with you and guide your steps.

While the noble man was still on the way, his servant met him with the news that his boy was still alive. When he enquired as to the time when his son got better, they said to him, "The fever left him yesterday at the seventh hour." (John 4: 52)

For the women facing these problems, look what happens when you believe his Word; life comes back into every dead situation. If you believe the promise of God, that whatever you ask, He has already done for you; then like the noble man, as you walk in faith you will find your reproductive organs perfected by a loving God in the name of His son, Jesus Christ.

Jesus at a wedding

The second Bible account I will like us to look into is found in John 2. This is an account of our Lord Jesus Christ at a wedding at Cana. Jesus at a wedding? Yes, Jesus goes to weddings, He is the God of marriage. Even today He still attends weddings when He is invited. If He is invited, He will come, He enjoys coming. Many of us have never thought of Jesus as one who will come to a wedding to enjoy it. We always think of Him as one who will come to perform a priestly duty - a superior pastor, well dressed-up and serious, bashing his Bible around. But that is not the Jesus I know.

Full Of Joy

The Jesus I know is the one full of joy who enjoys life, who delights in little children, who enjoys friendship. He enjoyed life so much that people called Him a glutton, a friend of sinners. All these were slanderous statements but the point is clear; they expected a Bible basher - what they saw outwardly was a down-to-earth saviour who loved life, who constantly cheered up people, who said to us, "Be of good cheer…" Why? - because He was happy. I have Him living in my home as the Lord of our home in the person of the Holy Spirit and every day we dance with all my family as we worship and praise Him in songs. The Jesus I am testifying to you is real. He brings happiness wherever He is invited.

What Happened At The Wedding

As this wedding progressed, the wine ran out. Jesus' mother was at the wedding also. She came to him and said, "They have no wine." This was indeed an embarrassing moment for this couple; from all indications the couple were a bit tight on money (poor). Can you imagine the shame especially for a young bride? I know what I would have felt if I were in their position.

For those of you women who faced the same embarrassing situation I also want to encourage you "Be of good cheer." No matter what the weakness is, Jesus is able to turn it into strength for you. The Bible says He works all things together for our good.

Jesus' action

In a moment Jesus had made a decision. He said to the servants who were there. "Fill the six water pots that were standing nearby with water." This they did. He then said to them, "Now draw some and take it to the master of the banquet." (John 2: 6-8) They obeyed Him and did what He commanded. The master of the feast tasted the water turned into wine and not knowing where it came from, asked the bridegroom. "Why did you keep the best wine till the last?"

For the women who face the above problems, I will advise you to tell Jesus what problems you may be facing. In an instant, without words, He saved this couple from shame. He can do the same for you. He has saved the best for you till last.

The God Of Marriage

What Jesus did at this marriage party (feast) shows us the kind nature of God. For the Bible says, "God was in Christ reconciling himself to the world." God loves weddings, God likes happiness. Here at the Cana wedding we see the eternal Christ - so human, so natural, happy in a little festive gathering of villagers, empathising with the joy of young lovers in their marriage. That to me is God. That is how God feels; God is interested in your marriage too.

For the woman who faces these problems I want you to know today that God cares; He wants to come into your home, bring you joy and peace, heal you and restore dignity into your life, bless you with children and even more. For this Cana couple, they ended up rich that day. Jesus left them with 180 gallons of choice wine, which they could sell. They could start their marital life together with money made from that sale. That is how thoughtful our Lord is. When He comes into your life, He brings super abundant blessings. Read more of this revelation in the early chapters covering female infertility and congenital disorders.

Invite Him Anyway

For those couples who face infertility due to the above-named problems, I would like to encourage you to invite God into your marriage. Marriage is no child's play. Without God as the third party in a marriage, it could become stale; unprofitable, unkind, and unloving. Having been married for some time now , I can testify that if not for Him I do not know what I could have done. His constant presence has sustained both my husband

and myself including our children in trying times. No amount of love is safe without God. After the partying is over, after the honeymoon, when the blinds are down, only God can make a difference in a marriage because He is the God of marriage.

Today, invite Jesus into your home, into your situation and let Him bring you joy and peace. Remember He loves and cares for you. These are some of His promises to you:

• I will uphold all those who fall and lift up all who are bowed down.

• I will open my hands and satisfy the desires of every living thing. (Psalms 145: 4)

• I will watch over the way of those who fear me. (Psalms 145: 20)

That is the God you are calling. He is faithful.

I want to link both Bible accounts together to encourage you to trust in the Lord and to know that He cares for you. In the first account, we see a noble man who faced the death of his only son. No human being alive could help Him, no money could buy back the life of that boy, but Jesus came into that situation and brought back joy and peace into it.

We see Him at the wedding turning water into wine to save a young couple from shame and embarrassment; in both cases we see the Lord intervening in family life, to make sure that joy and peace and honour are retained.

In your case, you mean just as much to God. His desire is to come into your home, heal you and leave you with joy and blessing as He did for this Cana couple.

Points Of Action

• Come to God by faith
• Tell Him all about the medical report you received from doctors.
• Ask Him to heal you.
• Obey Him by doing whatever He tells you to do.
• Believe and trust He has done it.
• Thank Him for it.
• Confess it out of your mouth.
• Keep praising God for it, no matter how the physical state may look.

This is what I know. "I know the Lord saves His anointed, He answers from His holy heaven, with the saving power of His right hand." (Psalms 20: 6)

Now make your confession:

Father, in Jesus' name I bless you. I come to you today with a heart of praise and gratitude. Father, I subject my ovaries to Your Word which is creative and energising. I command that your Word recreate any part of my ovaries that may be damaged or in need of recreative surgery.

I also command the powerful Word of God to energise and bring back to full operation any part of my ovaries that may have been destroyed by sickness or disease. I thank you father for my ovaries are working normally. All the defects that existed before have been dealt with by your Word which is powerful. The Father is rebuilding the old waste-places of my live, I'm like a green pine tree; my fruitfulness comes from the Father. (Hosea 14:8) All that the canker worm has eaten the Father is now restoring to me. My ovaries are working normally the way God ordained for it to work. Thank you Father in Jesus' name. Amen.

Chapter Eight

Idiopathic Infertility (infertility of unknown cause)

This is infertility from an unknown cause or unexplained. This is where all the tests and investigations have been carried out and yet no reason can be found medically as to why conception fails to occur.

The word *idiopathic* comes from the Greek word "idios", which means one's own and pathos meaning disease. Today, I would like to come into your home and just sit down over a glass of water with you, and, with the help of the Holy Spirit, just chat with you as a couple so that I can also give you some advice that will help you.

You say to me, "Veronica, we so much desire to conceive and have children; we have spent so much money going from one clinic to another; we have done all the tests the specialists recommend, yet, when all's said and done, the doctors have told us, 'Sorry, we can't help you, since we can't find any reason why both of you cannot conceive. Sorry, we have done our best for you. We wish you well and goodbye.'"

You have walked out of the clinic tired, drained financially and emotionally battered, defeated, bruised; a feeling of hopelessness and defeat sweeps over you. You come home, cry in each other's arms and then you say to one another, "There is no God; if there is a God, why does He allow such pain, such suffering and misery?" You cry a bit more, and then you sit down and yet again start planning what you are going to do next.

This is where I can help.

You are a healed person

I have come here to tell you that during my research for this book, I came across so many couples who have gone this route several times and yet they are not willing to give up. They are ready to try anything. One lady actually said she would keep trying till all the money she has saved up was gone; then she would consider other alternatives. But today, I bring good news to such couples. I know the one who can help you.His name is Jesus Christ, He is the one who created you and me; He is the one who died on the Cross to set us free from sin, from infertility and every other thing that tries to bind us. The Bible says that: "He took up our infirmities and carried our sorrows; he was pierced for our transgression, he was crushed for our iniquities.The punishment that brought us peace was upon him and by His wounds, we are healed. (Isaiah 53: 4-5) You are already a blessed and healed person.

From this passage you can see that all that pain and sorrow you have gone through was not necessary. Christ has already being pierced for you; you did not need to have your body pierced again by needles etc., or undergo so much pain. He Himself had already borne your pain and by His wounds you were healed. You are a healed person. No matter what pain you are going through, please believe me when I tell you that you are a healed person. Infertility has no right to torment you, in Jesus' name.

Jesus knows all things

The next thing I want to get clear is this statement made by the disciples of Jesus: "Now we see you know all things." (John 16: 30) Another statement that shows that Jesus knows all men is: "Jesus would not entrust himself to them, for he knew all men...for he knew what was in a man. (John 2: 24-25)

Only Jesus knows what is in a man. He knows what is wrong. He knows why you are not conceiving. He knows what to do and He is also able to correct the condition for you.

Before we continue, I will like to take us to the Bible to see a man who faced a similar situation like you for you to see what he did. I pray that the Holy Spirit will quicken your understanding as you read this and bring you a quick victory in Jesus' name.

President decides to trust God

What would you think if the president or leader of your country came on the TV network to confess, "We in this government don't know what to do any more; we are confused and have no further sense of direction."? What do you think the citizens would do?Answer that question yourself.

Yet, this is what Jehoshaphat did. Three enemy armies were closing in on Judah and this mighty leader called the nation together in Jerusalem to formulate a war plan. He needed to plan a decisive line of action. Something had to be done immediately; there was no time to be wasted. Instead, Jehoshaphat stood before his people and poured out his heart to God in confession. After praising God for His might and power, he said to God: "For we have no power to go and face this vast army that is attacking us. We do not know what to do but our eyes are upon you." (2 Chronicles 20: 12) What kind of war plan is that? - no programme, no board meeting, no war machines rolling out, nothing.

For those couples who face infertility of no known cause, I want to advise you today to stop running up and down. I want you instead to learn from what Jehoshaphat and his people did when they faced the enemy. Indeed you face a great enemy for I have already said that infertility is the enemy of God first, then of man. It is an enemy because it tries to make the command of God, which is for man to multiply, look like a lie. It is one enemy that you cannot fight on your own. You need God's help and His Word to defeat infertility.

Jehoshaphat decided to stand still, admit his confusion and helplessness in that situation, and put all their nation's eggs in one basket. They would not move anywhere but closer to their Lord; they would not look anywhere else for help but to Him.

Stop running around

I would advise you to decide right now that there will be no more running up and down, no more looking to the left or to the right. You are to make a decision; today we are going to trust God; we are going to look up to Him; we are going to cast all our cares upon Him for He cares for us; we are going to put all our eggs in one basket. This time our eyes are upon you, O God. When that baby comes, Lord, it has to come from you.

What this great king did will sound foolish to most people. A lot of people today feel they must help themselves and then God will help them. The urge to make things happen has robbed many people of great victories even among Christians. Oh, we must be planning this or giving this, or doing that, or else God will not be happy with us.

73

Admit your pain and confusion

This urge to make things happen contradicts the word of God which tells us to cast our cares upon the Lord for He cares for us. He tells us to look unto Jesus, the author and perfecter of our faith. He tells us, "Look unto me and be saved, all you ends of the earth; for I am God and there is no other." (Isaiah 45: 22) This is the biblical way to approach the problems of today. Put your hands up and say, "God, I don't know what to do but my eyes are upon you. I don't know what to do, but, Lord, you do know and I trust you to do the best for me in this situation."

I know about all the pains and hurts you two have gone through; I know of the suffering you have gone through but I also want to tell you that God loves you. God cares about you. When you hurt, God hurts; when you cry, He cries too. For the Bible says "...in all their distress he too was distressed." (Isaiah 63: 9)

His desire is for you to reach out to Him. This is what the Lord says: "He who made the earth, the Lord who formed it and established it, the Lord is his name. Call to me and I will answer you and tell you great and unsearchable things you do not know." (Jeremiah 33: 3)

God's telephone number

When I saw this passage of scripture in the Bible, it became my favourite scripture. The God of the whole world has given me His phone number - free access to Him without any time limit. He has also promised that at any hour you call, He will answer you. He has promised to show you great and unsearchable things that you do not know. Here is a definite promise to you that God will show you the cause of infertility and He will bless you but first, like Jehoshaphat, you must call Him. You now say, "How can I call God? Where is He?" Note how Jehoshaphat called Him: "Then Jehoshaphat stood up in the assembly of Judah and Jerusalem at the temple of the Lord in front of the new courtyard." (2 Chronicles 20: 5) He was in front of the courtyard of the temple when he started speaking to God.

I want to go to the Bible to show you passages to reassure you that God is omnipresent; He is everywhere. He can hear you from anywhere you call on Him.

Where can I go from your spirit, where can I flee from your presence? If I go to the heavens you are there, if I make my bed in the depths, you are there, if I rise on the wings of the dawn, if I settle on the far side of the sea, even there your hand will guide me, your right hand will hold me fast." (Psalms 139: 7-19)

Just call on God, It does not matter whether in the bath or in the car - anywhere; call on Him with sincerity of heart and He will answer you. As Jehoshaphat was crying out to God, He spoke back to the king and his people: "Listen King Jehoshaphat. This is what the Lord says to you: Do not be afraid or discouraged because of this vast army, for the battle is not yours, but God's." (2 Chronicles 20: 15) The king called unto his God and admitted he was helpless, then God stepped in to tell him not to worry because God Himself was the one who was going to fight the battle for him.

When you also come to God and as a couple agree that you are helpless and have decided to hand everything into God's hand, just watch and you will see what God will do for you. As God told the king: "Take up your positions, stand firm and see the deliverance the Lord will give you. Do not be afraid, do not be discouraged." (2 Chronicles 20: 17) God is saying the same thing to you - do not be afraid, my children, do not be discouraged; just take your position, stand firm and see what God will do for infertility.

What position did the king take? The Bible says: "Jehoshaphat bowed down with his face to the ground. Then some Levites from the Kohathites stood up and praised the Lord, the God of Israel, with a loud voice."

Victory through praise

As they began to sing praises, the Lord set ambushes against the men of Ammon and Moab and Mount Seir, who were invading Judah, and they were defeated. The men of Ammon and Moab rose up against the men of Mount Seir to destroy and annihilate them. After they finished slaughtering the men of Seir, they helped to destroy one another. (2 Chronicles 20: 22-23)

Even as you start to praise God, say to Him: "Great God, creator of the heavens and the earth, I give you thanks, for your love endures forever. I thank you, for the battle belongs to you; you will destroy infertility in our home and totally annihilate it in Jesus' name, as you did to the enemies of Jehoshaphat. We worship you, O God, we praise you." As you start to praise God, watch what He will do for you.

Praise is the Christians' weapon of war. When you start to praise God, every enemy that has risen up against you flees. There is nothing that can be compared to praising God - when you praise God, every chain of bondage falls away and victory comes your way. I would advise you to emulate this. Praise is the master key into the throne-room of God. The Bible commands us to come into God's gate with thanksgiving and into His courts with praise. (Psalms 100: 4) Give thanks to His name and praise Him. If you start to praise God now for His love and mercy and start to thank Him for His faithfulness, before you know it, things will change for you like it did for Jehoshaphat when he praised God.

"Then Jehoshaphat and all the men, of Judah and Jerusalem, returned joyfully to Jerusalem, for the Lord had given them cause to rejoice over their enemies." If you do what Jehoshaphat did, the God who said "I am no respecter of persons," who said "He does not change like shifting shadows," (James 1: 17), who said, " God does not show favouritism (Romans 2: 11), who said, "I am the Lord, I change not," will make your home a joyful place by bringing you the laughter and cry of a new baby. He is faithful.

The Bible actually says that God stoops down to bless you

The Bible says *Almighty* God stoops, to look upon those in heaven and on earth.

The seat of God almighty is so high that in order to behold the things in the heaven and on the earth, He has to humble himself, that is He has to stoop down. What is to stoop down? It means to bend the body forwards and downwards, sometimes simultaneously bending the knees; it can also mean to lower oneself morally. Thus the purpose of that stooping down is revealed; it is so that He may raise the poor and lift the needy. Then finally the Bible moves on to say, "...he settles the barren woman..." God thus stoops again to crown womanhood with motherhood.

The God who dwells in the heights above in the heavens, stooped through His love and grace, in His only begotten son, Jesus Christ, "(John 1: 18), in order that He might lift the needy. As He approached the ultimate depths in this stooping, He once again declared His intentions: "To settle the barren woman in her home as a happy mother of children." (Psalms 113: 6-9)

Praise the Lord.

I want to link both these Bible accounts to encourage you to hold on to God and His Word for it is forever true. First we see God intervene in the life of a nation to fight their battle when the king and his assistants did not know what to do. If you are in the same position and are helpless, if you ask God for help, He will surely step in to help and bring victory. Not only will He bring victory, He is ready to stoop down to the place where you are to bring that help. Oh, how much God loves you. Wipe your tears away and smile; the sun is shining for you today. Jesus has taken over, your victory is guaranteed. I have written down some points of action to help you as a guideline. Go to God in your own way and if you are sincere, He will surely help you. God bless you.

Points of action

- Come to God by faith.

- Tell Him about all the medical reports you have received from doctors.

- Tell Him you don't know what to do.

- Obey whatever He tells you to do.

- Believe and trust in Him that has done it.

- Thank Him for it.

- Confess it from your mouth.

- Keep praising God for it, no matter how the physical may look.

Confession

Father I thank you for your grace and mercy. I come to you today in the name of Jesus Christ and I bless you. I thank you that in Christ I am blessed and fruitful.

Father, I thank you that infertility is far from our home; we are blessed in Christ. Our home is full of the joy of the Lord and the blessings of the Lord which include children. Every hidden disorder in my body has been exposed and quickly dealt with by the living Word of God. I thank you Father, in Jesus' name that the curse of infertility is far from me.

Today I revoke and repent of any negative words I may have spoken in the past that may have bound my womb. I declare the victory of Christ in my life and I reject the very root of the curse of infertility. I am a mother of many children, I am like a fruitful vine in my husband's home.God grants me abundant prosperity in the fruit of my womb. God has removed savage beast from coming within my dwelling place. The sword of evil will not pass through my home. I pursue my enemy infertility and it falls by the sword before me.God looks on me with favour and makes me fruitful and increases my numbers. He keeps his covenant with me. While I am still recovering from last year's childbirth, it is time to make room for even more babies. God loves me. He walks with me. He has destroyed the yoke and bars infertility in my life and has enabled me to carry healthy babies in my womb and have perfect heaven ordained deliveries with my head held high. (Leviticus 26:3-13). In the name of Jesus I am blessed and highly favoured. Amen.

This one thing I know for sure; if almighty God will stoop, then for sure He will bless you even more than you ever thought or imagined. God bless you.

Chapter Nine

What The Word Of God Can Do In Our Life And Body

For the Word of God, "... is living and active, sharper than any double-edged sword. It judges the thoughts and attitude of the heart, it penetrates even to the diving soul and spirit, joints and marrow. Nothing in all creation is hidden from God's sight. Everything is uncovered and laid bare before the eyes of him to whom we must give account." (Hebrews 4: 12-13).

For the Word that God speaks is alive and full of power (making it active, operative, energising and effective). It is sharper than any two-edged sword, penetrating to the dividing line of the breath of life (soul) and (Immortal) spirit and of joints and marrow (of the deepest parts of our nature), exposing and sifting and analysing and judging the very thoughts and purpose of our hearts. And not a creature exist that is concealed from His sight, but all things are open and exposed, naked and defenceless to the eyes of Him to whom we must give account (Hebrews 4: 12-13).

The Word Of God Is Powerful

God's Word is powerful and covers a lot of problems and other things we meet or face from day to day. It is still:

Alive:

Having life still in existence, in force or in operation, active. The Word of God has life in it. Our Lord Jesus Christ said, "the words that I speak to you they are spirit and life." He came to the grave of Lazarus, a man who was dead four days and He called out in a loud voice "Lazarus, come out," and the dead man came out. His hands and feet were still wrapped with strips of linen and a cloth was round his face. But our Lord's words were put to action and it worked. (John 11: 43-44)

Active:

Characterised by practical action rather than by contemplation or speculation. The Word of God takes an interest and makes quick physical movement. It is lively, marked by vigorous activity, it is practical and is capable of taking an action on its own initative when activated. The Word of God does not waste time contemplating or speculating on what to do. Rather It takes a quick intrest in the situation and quickly apply practical solutions to it, bringing in a quick, active and positive change into that situation.

Sharp:

Adapted to cutting or piecing, e.g. having a thin, keen edge or fine point. Keen in intellect, perception, attention. Capable of action or reacting strongly. Cutting in language or implication. Affecting the senses or sense organs intensely. Clear in outline or detail. The Word of God is sharp and can be used in a situation where a tumour or growth needs to be sharply cut away from an organ of the body. Because of its sharp nature, it is capable of performing an operation and cutting through any form of growth or disease without any damage to the organ involved or risk to the life of the person it is operating on.

Quick:

Fast in understanding, thinking or learning, mentally agile, reacting with speed and keen. Fast in developing or in occurrence, for example a succession of events done or taking place with rapidity. Marked by speed, readiness or promptness of physical movement. Inclined to hastiness, e.g. in action or response to find fault. Capable of being easily and speedily prepared.

This I have experienced time and time again. While writing this chapter, I went shopping one evening and while coming back I was singing and praising God, and along comes this old man, shuffling along with his dog. He stopped and said to me: "Why are you so happy?" I replied that my happiness was about Jesus Christ who fills my heart with joy. He asked me to tell him more about Jesus Christ, because He was a good man but did not know who Jesus was. I stood there and explained to him who Christ is. He decided He wanted the Lord Jesus Christ in his life. I prayed with him there and he received salvation. He told me he had no kneecap and had endured six operations on his back and was due for the seventh one. I laid my hands on him and prayed for him and I asked God to create new kneecaps and heal his back. In less than the few minutes it took me to pray for him, he could bend down which was something he could not do before. I praise God for that.

The Bible says the Word of God is quick, fast in understanding, thinking, reacting with speed and keen in sensitivity. Marked by speed, and rapid physical movement, while doctors are busy taking x-rays or all sorts of tests, the Word of God has quickly and speedily finished off what needs to be done, because it takes a quick interest in any situation and quickly and promptly brings a solution to it.

Exposed:

To deprive of shelter or protection, lay open to attack or influence. To subject to an action or influence, to subject to action of radiant energy. To lay open to view, to display, e.g. to exhibit for public veneration. To bring shamefully to light.

The Word of God exposes every hidden thing. How many times have you seen a sick person tell you they are sick and yet after medical investigation no one can detect what is wrong with them? Not so with the Word of God. The Word of God deprives disease of shelter in our bodies. He lays every hidden sickness open for attack and subject to the power that is in His Word. He stripes open to view every hidden disease, bringing it shamefully to light.

Judges:

A judge forms a judgement or opinion about any given situation. The Word of God is a judge. God left His Word on earth to be judge for us in all life situations. Who is a Judge? A judge is somebody who judges, e.g. a public official authorised to decide questions brought before a court. Somebody who gives an authoritative opinion. The Word of God is able to form an opinion, to make a decision as soon as it is applied to a situation. It is able to give an authoritative opinion on every issue or situation in life. Be it physical or spiritual, because it is a Judge. This is a good scripture for those with infertility of unknown cause, the Word of God judges and quickly gives a decision on the issue. And the decision is always based on the truth of Gods Word.

Living:

The Word of God has life in it. It is alive.

Operative:

Producing an appropriate effect. The Word of God exacts power or influences situations or factors operating against us. It influences sickness, disease, or anything standing in the way of our success. It produces a desired effect.

The Word of God performs surgery. Yes, the Word of God is capable of performing major or minor operations, without the person being cut or suffering any pain. The surgery done is to bring about or cause any organ or part of our bodies to function, or be put in normal operation the way God ordained it to function in Jesus' name.

If we put our faith into action and believe God, He will surely make what we are beliving Him for come true.

Energising:

To give energy to, to make energetic or vigorous, to apply energy so as to facilitate normal operation. The Word of God energises. The Word of God is able to give energy, make vigorous any situation or any part of the body that could be dead. It is able, when applied in faith, to bring back life and facilitate normal operation of any part of the body that may be impotent - you can, by applying the Word of God, receive life back in any affected part of the body, or any life situation that needs a resurrection.

Analyse:

To subject to analysis, to determine the constitution or structure of a thing. The Word of God is able to analyse any problem and form an immediate opinion about it.

In the next chapter we will be using the analysies from the word of God to bring healing to those who face infertility of unknown cause.

Chapter Ten

How To Avoid Unnecessary Tests And Treatment When Having Difficulty In Conceiving

If you as a couple have being trying to conceive for more than a year without any result, if sexual intercourse has been taking place normally, and no pregnancy shows up, or if you suspect either of you have a problem not yet identified by the doctors, and you desire to avoid all the hassles of infertility treatment, this is what you can do. I'm not advising you not to go to your doctor, please, but any woman who has gone through all the fertility tests will tell you that it is not a pleasant experience. However, what you do is your personal choice and decision.

Here is my suggestion to you based on the Word of God. You have to speak to your body. Remember the chapter on the power of your own words. The Bible says "the lips of the wise protect them." (Proverbs 14: 3) This means that if you choose to be wise now you will protect yourself from suffering and pain and save thousands of pounds which infertility treatment will cost you. The Word of God says that the tongue that brings healing is a tree of life (Proverbs 15: 4), which means your own words can bring healing into your body when you line them up with God's Word. Let's look at some of the medical investigation you will undergo when you go to the infertility clinic for testing.

Medical investigations to discover the cause of infertility

Women

Females take a menstrual history, which includes a study of body temperature during the menstrual cycle, as this gives an indication of the time of ovulation. There is a blood and urine test to discover whether ovulation is normal.

Body Temperature And Ovulation

Charting a woman's body temperature during her menstrual cycle can indicate abnormalities of ovulation.

Hysterosalpingoo-ography

This is an x-ray technique used to visualise the uterus and Fallopian tubes to determine whether or not there is any abnormality.

Laparoscopy

With this technique, a laparoscopy (a type of viewing tube) is inserted through the abdominal wall to examine the woman's reproductive organs and determine whether an abnormality, such as a cyst or tumour, is present.

Having looked at the medical side of the investigation, this will normally be done at the fertility clinic when you go for a test. We now go straight into the Word of God. In dealing with this we are going to be picking from the analysis from Hebrews 4: 12 on what the Word of God does in our body.

Women's confession

This is how you will apply the Word to your reproductive organs.

> Father, I thank you and praise you in Jesus' name. I take your Word which is quick, sharp, effective, energising, operative, analysing and now I speak to my reproductive system.

The Word of God to analyse & energise the following:

My Vagina and cervix

In the mighty name of Jesus I ask the Word of God to analyse my vagina and my cervix and if any weakness or hidden disorder exists, I command the Word of God to restore and renew these parts in the name of Jesus. If there is any part of my cervix or vagina that needs energising; I Praise the Word of God for energising those parts in the name of Jesus. I thank you Father that all my reproducive organ are working the way you ordained them to work in Jesus'name. My vagina and cervix is strong and strenghtend by the power of Your Word. Thank You Father in Jesus' name. Amen.

The Word of God to analysis and operate on my womb

I subject my uterus to the Word of God and command in Jesus' name that it be analysed and if any abnormality exists which may prevent the implantation of a fertilised egg, I ask the Word of God to operate and destroy any planting in my womb that is not of God. I ask the Word of God to create the right environment that will sustain the life of the baby the Father has blessed me with in Jesus' name. Amen.

Energise my ovaries

I speak to my ovaries; if there is any reason why my eggs fail to mature or may not be released, I command in Jesus' name that the Word of God begin to energise those ovaries to facilitate normal operation in Jesus' name.

Analyse and operate on my Fallopian Tube

I speak to my Fallopian tubes in Jesus' name, I subject those tubes to the analysing power of God's Word; nothing in all creation is hidden from God's sight, If any blockage or damage exists that could prevent the sperm reaching the egg, or if one or both of my tubes are blocked, in Jesus' name I command that the Word of God operate and unblock those tubes and make them function normally in Jesus' name. I thank you Father that my tubes can now transport life in Jesus name. Amen.

A prayer on your behalf for anyone looking for a child

Father, in the name of Jesus Christ, I pray for my sister under the authority you have given me, I pray that, as she confess your Word into her body, that your Word will bring light and dispel darkness. I stand in agreement with her that you will grant her the desires of her heart in Jesus' name. Amen.

Good news: I gave this confession to a friend who had been trying to conceive - while this book was being edited. Now she is pregnant.

Chapter Eleven

You Are Not Too Old To Conceive

In this chapter we are going to be looking at the issue of childbirth for the older woman, from God's perspective. This issue is a very delicate subject to many, so we are going to invite the Holy Spirit to take control of it straight away.

Under the clear leadership of the Holy Spirit we are going to go into the Word of God to see what God has to tell His women who have been told by their doctors that they are too old to conceive.

Looking at the issue from a medical perspective, we will first look at what happens to a woman, from the time she is conceived to when she reaches child-bearing age.

Medical background (Fertilisation and beginning of a new life)

When sexual intercourse takes place and an egg is fertilised, if the fertilised egg is a female embryo, after twenty-one days, it starts to develop within it a group of cells which specialise and become her ovaries. Initially only a group of some one hundred cells. The primitive ovary moves into position within the embryo and starts to grow. At their peak the ovaries will contain a few million egg cells, and the numbers are already starting to decline, even before birth. The surviving cells are immature and they need to wait patiently for thirteen or more years until the girl reaches puberty. At this point, only half a million or less will still be present of which some four or five hundred may be released, and only a handful of these will ever be fertilised and grow into babies.

NOTE: After the birth of a female child, her ovaries do not produce new eggs, so any damage or accident, or exposure to radiation, and a girl's ovaries may never release a viable egg. Furthermore, eggs released at the end of a woman's reproductive life come from cells that have waited some forty or fifty years.

What Happens At Puberty

At puberty, a pea-sized gland, the pituitary gland, becomes active, lying just under the brain, and five centimetres behind the eyes. It starts releasing hormones into the bloodstream which activates cells in the ovaries.

Monthly Menstrual Cycle

A woman releases an egg once every month. At the same time, her body needs to prepare to receive an embryo, should intercourse occur, and the egg is fertilised. There is a circle of events that happens to ensure that the egg is released just when the lining of the womb is best prepared to receive an embryo.

(a)   Follicle-stimulating hormone from the pituitary stimulates a few eggs to start developing in the ovaries.

(b)   Soon one egg starts to outgrow all the others, and as it does, the other cells die.

(c)   Next, cells surrounding the growing cell form a blister-like pocket, a follicle.

(d)   The follicle cells release the female hormone, oestrogen, into the blood stream.

(e)   The oestrogen released into the bloodstream acts on the lining of the womb, causing it to thicken and be ready to accept an embryo.

f)   The rising oestrogen now sends a stimulus to the area of the brain called the hypothalamus informing it that the egg is ready to be released.

(g)   The hypothalamus sends signals to the pituitary to stop producing FSH and, for two days, to release another hormone, called Luteinizing hormone (LH). This causes the egg to finish

maturing, and some thirty-six hours after LH release starts,
the follicle bursts, releasing the egg; ovulation has occurred.

(h)   The corpus luteum: When ovulation occurs, the LH also makes the follicle develop into corpus luteum (CL). This produces a hormone called progesterone that continues to maintain the lining of the womb, preventing a menstrual period and thereby preventing the embryo from being washed away.

(i)   HCG: If a pregnancy occurs, the embryo produces human chorionic gonadotrophin (HCG), a hormone that is very similar to LH. This causes the corpus luteum to remain, maintaining the lining of the womb.

(j)   If the egg is not fertilised, or if it is fertilised but fails to implant in the lining of the womb, it is washed away. No HCG is produced and consequently the CL dies away and the progesterone level falls. Deprived of progesterone, the blood vessel in the uterine lining contracts, starving the tissue of oxygen. Rapidly the cells die and the lining of the womb starts to break up, and be shed. A period has begun.

(k)   In a few days the lining has been lost, and again the brain sends signals to the anterior pituitary gland which results in the release of more FSH. The cycle continues.

This is what happens from when a girl is born to puberty and when she reaches menstruation and child-bearing age.

Why do they say you are too old to conceive?

Most women between the ages of thirty-five to fifty years have been told they are too old to conceive. The reason given for this medically is mostly due to:

a)   Lack of egg production

b)   Menopause: lack of menstruation

The Menopause

What is it? It simply means to stop the menstrual period. This is referred to by some people as the change.

METHODS OF FEMALE STERILIZATION

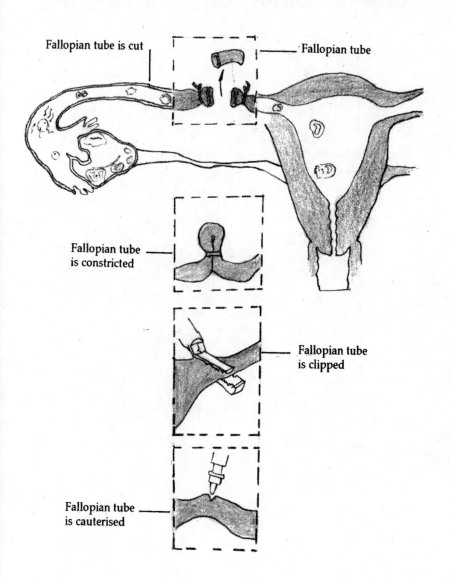

Fallopian tube is cut

Fallopian tube

Fallopian tube is constricted

Fallopian tube is clipped

Fallopian tube is cauterised

LOCATION OF AN ECTOPIC PREGNANCY

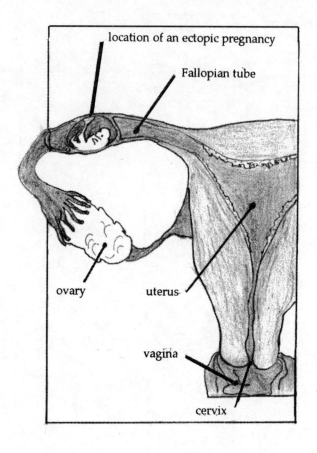

location of an ectopic pregnancy

Fallopian tube

ovary

uterus

vagina

cervix

PICTURE OF THE CERVIX ILLUSTRATING GROWTHS THAT OCCUR IN THE CERVIX AREA

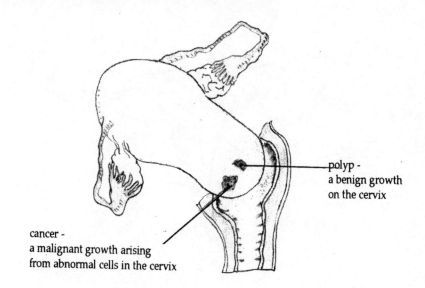

polyp -
a benign growth
on the cervix

cancer -
a malignant growth arising
from abnormal cells in the cervix

LOCATION OF FIBROIDS

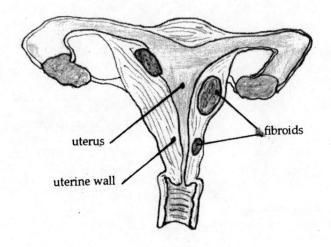

FERTILIZATION BEGINNING OF A NEW LIFE

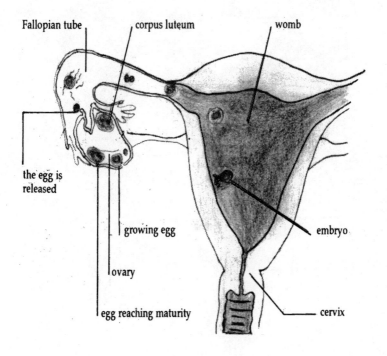

Fallopian tube

corpus luteum

womb

the egg is
released

growing egg

embryo

ovary

egg reaching maturity

cervix

FEMALE REPRODUCTIVE ORGAN

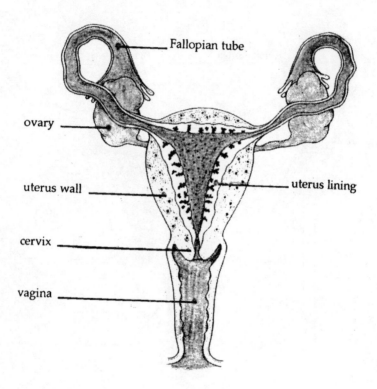

Fallopian tube

ovary

uterus wall

uterus lining

cervix

vagina

A PICTURE OF THE FEMALE REPRODUCTIVE ORGANSSHOWING SITES OF ENDOMETRIOSIS

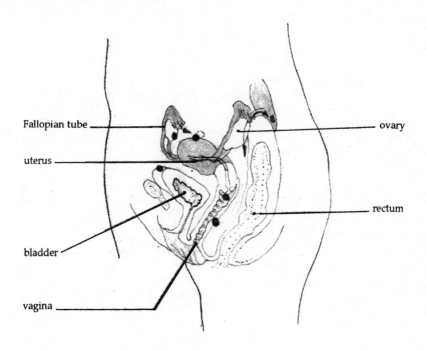

Fallopian tube — ovary

uterus

rectum

bladder

vagina

Fragments of the endometrium may travel from the uterus into the plevic area through the fallopian tubes. They then implant on parts of the pelvic organs (such as the ovaries, vagina, cervix, bladder, and rectum).

It is a period of change in a woman's life, where a complex of symptoms and bodily changes take place, some due to failing production of oestrogen and some due to other factors.

Medically, the answer to why the menopause happens is not clear. When some women reach this phase in their lives, menstruation stops, and they pass into the next phase. Some women show many signs and symptoms of oestrogen deficiency and respond well to having this state explained to them.

In discussing the menopause here, we are not talking about premature menopause - that happens to younger women. We are discussing, in general, the older woman.

During this period, the woman's ovaries are failing. Their function is declining. So the ovary which contained over a million eggs at birth, now has about 5000-6000 left. Over the next few years the number continues to decrease until none, or only a few, remain.

During these last few years, the remaining eggs become increasingly unresponsive to the hormones of the pituitary. The menstrual cycles which may occur, are more often not ovulating, that is, there is no egg production in the middle of the cycle. This whole process may take one to five years or even longer. It is complete when the function of the ovary finally ceases, between the ages of thirty-eight to fifty years. This age varies.

NOTE: It is important to note that the production of oestrogen does not completely stop. Other sources of oestrogen remain and the main one is through the conversion of the hormone adrostenedione into oestrogen.

Having listed briefly some of the medical reasons why a woman could be too old to conceive, we will go into the Bible to see what God did for two older couples who faced this problem. (Note: you will read a lot about "a righteous man" in this chapter - this refers to both men and women)

While researching for this book, I discovered that age does not affect men's fertility as it does women's. I would advise the men to go and get my men's book " *Man You Are Not Infertile*" which I belive will be a blessing to you and remember, I love you all you wonderful men of God, so do not say, "She is being a woman now!" God bless you.

First we will be meeting two older couples from the Bible. The first couple is:-

Abraham and Sarah

Now Sarah, Abraham's wife, had borne him no children (Genesis 16: 1).

Abraham and Sarah's medical report - from the Bible (Romans 4: 18-19)

Abraham was impotent. He could not make love any more. All his reproductive organs were dead. Sarah, on the other hand, had passed child-bearing age, with the possibility of her having a child rated zero.

He did not weaken in faith when he considered the (utter) impotence of his own body, which was as good as dead, because he was about a hundred years old or (when he considered) the barrenness of Sarah's (deadened) womb.

Now we are going to take the facts of this case and deal with them one by one. The Bible says that Abraham's body was as good as dead, with Sarah's position being similar.

The fact of the matter was that this couple's reproductive system had ceased to work normally, they were past child-bearing age, but still we will look at what God did and what they did.

First we see a man who is a hundred years old and his wife who is ninety years old. No doctor on earth will even talk to such people about having children. What we see here are the medical facts of this case. This was really an impossibility. They themselves could not deny the fact that their bodies were dead. Today, even women as young as forty-five years are told they are too old to conceive and some doctors will not consider them for fertility treatment. Most of them have to pay a lot of money for fertility treatments, without any hope of it succeeding.

While this couple were running up and down, trying to conceive; God now comes along with a promise to let them know that with Him all things are possible. Let's look at the Word of God to them.

The promise itself

When Abraham was ninety-nine years old, the Lord appeared to him and said, "I am God almighty, walk before me and I will greatly increase your numbers." (Genesis 17: 1-2)

God also gave Abraham this promise regarding Sarah his wife:

> "I will bless her and surely give you a son by her. I will bless her so that she will be the mother of nations, kings of people will come from her." Abraham fell face down, he laughed and said to himself, "Will a son be born to a man a hundred years old? Will Sarah bear a child at the age of ninety?" (Genesis 17: 15-17)

> God said to him (Abraham), "As for me, this is my covenant with you. You will be the father of many nations. No longer will you be called Abram. Your name will be Abraham, for I have made you a father of many nations. I will make nations of you and kings will come from you."

When God gave this couple this promise, He did not say to them, "Abraham go and look for a man at the fertility clinic to donate sperm for you to impregnate your wife." God did not say to Sarah, "Go and see who you can pay to have eggs donated to you, or who will lend a womb to you by carrying your baby because you are so old. Or go for IVF - let the doctors mix Abraham's sperm and your eggs in a glass and try to make a child for you."

God told them they were going to have fun making that baby; they were going to have pleasure, have the child in the way ordained by God, for the next time the angel of God came to Abraham, Sarah was listening at the entrance to the tent, which was behind him. Abraham and Sarah were already old and well advanced in years, and Sarah was past the age of child-bearing. So she laughed to herself as she thought, "After I am worn out and my master is old, will we now have this pleasure?" Then the Lord said to Abraham, "Why did Sarah laugh and say, 'Will I really have a child, now that I am old?' Is anything hard for the Lord? I will return to you at the appointed time next year and Sarah will have a son." (Genesis 18: 10-14)

We read in Sarah's words her response to God's promise; she could not comprehend how she would make love at one hundred years of age.

The promise is by faith

"After I am worn out and my master is old, will we now have this pleasure?" She did not think it was possible for her and Abraham to make love any more but God's Word is true and sure. They had a promise bigger than the problem.

The Bible says that the promise comes by faith, so that it may be by grace and may be guaranteed to all Abraham's offspring. Not only those who are of the law, but also to those who are of the faith of Abraham. He is the father of us all. This promise is for every woman who is old and yet by faith believe the Word of God. The promise is greater than the situation.

When all the doctors and specialists in the world had told Abraham and Sarah that they could not have children, they switched from the report of the doctors who were giving them no hope. They took their hope from the Word of God and put it in the place of the hopelessness given them by the medical reports.

Abraham and Sarah put their faith on top of hope

Abraham hoped in faith, not in human reason, that he should become the father of many nations, as he had been promised, "...so numberless shall your descendants be." Before we continue, let us find out what the dictionary says to hope means.

What does to hope mean? it means to wish with expectation of fulfilment, to long for with expectation, to expect with desire. Hope against hope, to hope without any basis for expecting fulfilment. The Bible says he put his "hope on faith; against all hope" Abraham hoped and believed and so became the father of many nations, just as it had been said to him, by He who gave him this promise. Abraham counted God faithful to fulfil His promise to him and his faith rested on the truth that God is able to do what He said He would do.

Here, in effect, the Bible is saying that, from the human point of view, every reason for hope was gone. This is the account of Abraham's mental attitude as a result of the promise of God to him. This demonstrates the expectation of good things to come with a corresponding activity towards the realisation of them. There could be no hope where there were no grounds for Abraham to expect that he should have an heir. The facts absolutely denied the possibility; nevertheless he hoped on the promise of God. He believed in God, God's promise was sufficient; therefore he hoped and expected that the prophesy would happen and he ordered his life accordingly. This is the very genius of the life of faith. All the great things we look at sometimes in our life may be humanly impossible but with God the impossible becomes possible.

The journey toward God's day

If we were to compute the possibilities, the realistic expectation upon the basis of things seen, this was the most hopeless of enterprises for the bringing to birth of the new order; the man's reproductive organs was dead and the woman was barren but if we reckon with God then we can be the most hopeful. He has promised and no Word of his can be void of power; therefore we hope against hope when there are no grounds for expectation in certain circumstances; we find the solution in God and so with jubilant songs we cheer through the night and journey towards the day of God.

The fulfilment of the promise. God's day

And the Bible continues that. "The Lord was gracious to Sarah as he had said, and the Lord did for Sarah what he had promised. Sarah became pregnant and bore a son to Abraham in his old age, at the very time God had promised him. Abraham was a hundred years old when his son Isaac was born to him, Sarah was ninety-one years old."

Sarah said, "God has brought me laughter, and every one who hears about this will laugh with me." And she added, "Who would have said to Abraham that Sarah would nurse children? Yet I have borne him a son in his old age. (Genesis 21: 1-6)

Here we see a couple, who were almost 100 years old, being told by God that they would be parents. Abraham and his wife laughed at God. They thought God was joking by telling geriatrics like them they would be parents but as we see in Genesis, Chapter 21, God's Word came to pass and that child was born. The child was n ot born with any genetic disorder or any problem for mother or child.

If God did it for them He can do it for you.

Flourishing in the courts of our God

The other Bible promise for the older person, comes from Psalm 92.

> The righteous will flourish like a palm tree, they will grow like a cedar of Lebanon; planted in the house of the Lord,

93

they will flourish in the courts of our God. They will still bear fruit in old age, they will stay fresh and green proclaiming, "the Lord is upright, he is my rock, and there is no wickedness in him." (Psalm 92: 12-15)

Can you better the Word of God? You see, His promise is clear. A woman who trusts in Him can still bear fruit in old age. God compares her productivity to that of the palm tree and the cedar tree. Let us take a brief look at the palm tree and how it flourishes.

The palm tree

The silhouette of the palm tree, with its tall slender unbranching trunk, surmounted by a wonderful crown of enormous leaves, is a sight which one could never forget or fail to recognise at first glance. The trunk stretches up, straight into the air, often for 100 feet or more, suddenly bursting at the top into a rosette of leaves radiating from it like the outspread fingers of the hand. It is this resemblance that gives the palm tree its name, taken from the Latin Word, *palma*, meaning, "palm of the hand".

There are over 1,200 species of the palm. It begins to bear fruit after six or eight years of planting, and can continue to be productive for a century. The leaves of some species can be twenty feet in length, droop slightly at the ends and whisper musically in the breeze. The palm tree is in truth, a beautiful and most useful tree.

The uses of the fruits of the palm tree

The palms are the most useful of all plants. Their fruits, stems, and leaves are used in a great number of manufactured products. Beside furnishing, food, shelter, and clothing (for the natives of the regions in which they abound), the palm tree gives shade from the sun.

Some palm products are:

(a)   Palm oil is derived from the fruits of the oil palm (Elccis guineensis), while other species are used for food. It is also used in:

(b)   Soap making; and as a lubricant.

(c)   Palm wine comes from the sap of several species.

(d)   Sago comes from the pith of the sago palm (matroxy ion), and other varieties.

(e)   Rattan comes from the thin flexible stems of various species of

D'Calamus.

(f)   Vegetable Ivory: the nuts of the Tagua or Ivory Palm,
(Phytelephas Macrocarpa) are used for the manufacture of
buttons and many other small articles. Many valuable fibres
are used in making brushes, hats, mats, and baskets are also
made from palms. Some of the commonest kinds are raffia,
plasava, kitool, African fibre, palmetto, and coir or Coconut
fibre. (from the *Book of Knowledge, Volume 6*).

In the Pacific Islands, the Coconut kernel, called Copra, is the chief
article of the island's trade, often taking the place of money in business
transactions.

In Syria, they have about 360 different uses to which the palm can
be put.

God's plan for you

God compares the productivity of the righteous to the palm tree and
the cedar tree. The palm tree has over 360 different uses and the cedar
tree bears fruit and thrives in barren land.God compares you to these
trees and still you are listening to lies from these people telling you that
you can't have children, that you are barren, too old, out of date. If you
are out of date, you will not have the desire to have children any more.
As long as that desire is alive in you, and if you hold on to God, He will
bless you.

Today I will advise you to stop thinking that you are useless and fruitless
and take the place which God has allotted to you. The Bible says that, "as
a man thinketh in his heart, so is he." (Proverbs 23: 7) So whatever you
allow to occupy your thoughts is what you will become.

The Holy Spirit enlightened me to this in the book of Ruth, where we
meet Naomi who was a very old woman. She said these words to her
daughter-in-laws, "I am too old to have another husband. Even if I
thought there was still hope for me - even if I had a husband tonight and
then gave birth to sons, would you wait until they grow up? Would you
remain unmarried for them?" (Ruth 1: 12-13)

Here we see a very old woman, talking about her fertility, and her
only limitation she admitted was her thoughts. If you can change your
thought patterns, you can have all you ever desired because "as a man
thinketh so is he." The Bible says you can wrestle with your thoughts
(Psalms 13: 2) What is to wrestle? The dictionary says it is to contend
with an opponent in wrestling, to engage in a violent or determined

struggle; you can engage in a wrestle with your thoughts, have a determined struggle till you get your thoughts in line with God's way and his Word. Any thought not in line with God's plan for you is an opponent. But the Bible says you can contend with that opponent and overcome it through Christ Jesus.

It flourishes

The palm tree is a fruitful tree, with perpetually green foliage; the height at which the foliage grows is as far as possible from the earth and as close as possible to the heavens. The elasticity of the fibre of the palm, and its determined growth upward, even when loaded with weights is extraordinary - the palm tree grows from within.

The palm tree and the righteous

There is no useless part in the palm tree. Every bit of the palm tree is useful.

So also are the **righteous** - those who have right-standing with God, through the blood that Jesus shed on the Cross for us. The Bible says that:

> The righteousness from God comes through faith in Jesus Christ to all who believe. (Romans 3: 22)

There is no useless part in the righteous person, for as you live and serve God, the Bible says, "The righteous flourish and prosperity will abound till the moon is no more." (Psalms 72: 7) Here our Lord Jesus is saying that as long as we remain in Him, we will keep bearing fruit and prospering all the days of our lives.

The palm tree grows from within - the righteous change from within

The work God does in the righteous is done within, through the Holy Spirit who lives in the believer. The ability to change our ways and accept the things of God is an internal work done within by the Holy Spirit.

The perpetual greenness of the palm tree

The perpetual greenness of its foliage also compares with the promise of God to believers, that in Christ:

> The righteous shall flourish and be fruitful at a ripe old age.
> (Psalms 92: 14)

> Blessed is the man who trusts in the Lord, whose confidence
> is in him. He will be like a tree planted by the water that
> sends out its roots by the stream. It does not fear when heat
> comes; its leaves are always green. It has no worries in a
> year of drought and never fails to bear fruit. (Jeremiah 17: 8)

Bears burden well

Note the elasticity of the fibre of the palm, and its determination
to grow upward, even when loaded with weights, like a righteous
person.

The daily persecution faced by the righteous will not deter such a
person from looking heaven-ward, towards a God Who has promised in
His Word that, "Many are the afflictions of the righteous, but the Lord
delivers him from all of them. He protects all his bones, not one of them
will be broken. (Psalms 34: 19-20)

The date palm was grown four thousand years ago along the Euphrates
and Tigris rivers, where it was too hot and too dry for other plants to
grow. The date palm flourished, and during all these centuries it has
blessed the natives with its fruits, its timber, and its cooling shade, under
which they can live and mature their orchards and vineyards.

Many desert parts of Arabia and the Sahara would not be habitable
were it not for this tree, which grows in their oases, and which is the
most important food plant of the great deserts.

God actually ordained that the righteous rule the earth. Full of His
wisdom, they are to be a shelter for the needy of the world, bringing
solution to all the problems in the world. The world would not be habitable
today, if not for the faithful prayers of the righteous. God's will is for a
righteous woman to be healthy and productive into ripe old age. God's
will is to bless the older woman who serves Him with children and
make her an example in the world where it is has become strange and
difficult for an older woman to have children. Age has never been an
issue with God when it comes to having children. Not once is it mentioned
in the Bible that an older woman will have difficulty conceiving. Rather
we see God bless so many older women with children in the Bible as an

example and testimony to His glory.

The comparison of the righteous man with the palm tree is a most powerful one. Just as the palm tree remains alive and is able to flourish in a hot and dry land:

God restores all the losses of the righteous

He promises to be with the righteous in trouble, to deliver and honour him "With long life will I satisfy him and show him my salvation." (Psalms 91: 15) The righteous person is able in Christ, to flourish and bear children, no matter what they may have gone through. Even when such a person has lost all their reproductive organs, God is able to recreate any missing part, to enable a righteous person to flourish and bear fruit even at ripe old age. The Bible says, "the righteous will hold onto their ways, and those with clean hands will grow stronger." (Job 17: 9)

Renewed like the eagle

Another powerful promise is from Psalm 103: 5: "…who satisfies your desires [your necessities and desire at your own particular age and in your own particular situation] with good things so that your youth is renewed like the eagle's [strong, overcoming, soaring].

The Bible states that at your personal age - the age at which you are now, and also the situation which you are now in - that Almighty God will satisfy your desire. No matter what it is, be it new reproductive organs, a baby, whatever your desire is for *now*. God has promised to satisfy you with good things. He also promises that you will be strong, able to overcome and able to soar. Let's look at these words: *strong* - having or marked by great physical power, having great resources of wealth, talent, etc. As a child of God you are a strong woman, having all the attributes of strength in your life.

You are also able to *overcome*. What is to overcome? - to get the better of or surmount difficulties, to overpower, overwhelm, to gain superiority, to win. The Bible says you, woman of God, you are supposed to overwhelm the situation; because you are superior to it, you are destined to win over infertility even at a ripe old age.

You are supposed to be able to *soar*. What is to soar? - to fly high in the air, to sail or hover in the air, at a great height, to fly without engine power and without loss of altitude, to rise rapidly to a very high position, to be of imposing height, to tower. God created you to be imposing, to fly at very high altitude, even without engine power. You are created to be imposing, to be of great height and stature, so take your place and say no to infertility.

Secondly, your youth is renewed like the eagle's. How does the eagle renew its youth?

The eagle, the king of birds

Let's take a brief look at the eagle - soaring high in the sky, or swooping down like a thunderbolt on the hopeless prey it has sighted from afar. The eagle well deserves its reputation as "the king of birds." The extraordinary power of sight, the terrifying majesty of its appearance, and the wild grandeur of the scenery in which the eagle loves to focus its eyes, have made it the universal emblem of might and courage from ancient times.

The eagle draws great lines across the sky. He sees the forest, like a carpet beneath him. He sees the hills and valleys and fields as patterns in a many-coloured tapestry. He sees the river as a silver belt, connecting remote horizons. He climbs mountain peaks to get a glimpse of the spectacle that is hourly spread out beneath him. Dignity, elevation, repose, are his.

Man is created to be "king"

God created man to be king on earth. Lets look at Psalms 8: 4-8:

> "What is man that you are mindful of him, the son of man that you care for him? You made him a little lower than the angels [yourself] and crowned him with glory and honour. You made him ruler over the works of your hands; you put everything under his feet: all flocks and herds, and the beasts of the field, the birds of the air, and the fish of the sea, all that swim the paths of the sea.

God created the righteous a little lower than himself, not lower than angels as this translation says. Man is an image of God and not in the image of an angel. God gave mankind authority over all He created. He gave us power and authority to rule on earth; the eagle has taken its place, it's time for us to take our own place on earth - the place of dignity, elevation, and repose. Let's look at the meaning of these words.

Dignity

The quality of being worthy, honoured or esteemed, belonging to high rank, office or position.

In the sight of God you have love, respect and dignity, you are honourable to God; don't let any circumstance of life take you away from where God has placed you.

Repose

To lay at rest, head on the cushion, to lie resting.

He has given you rest from all of life's limitation, for He said, "Do not let your hearts be troubled, I have overcome the world." Everything that limits you from becoming a mother has been overcome by the death of Christ on the Cross and His resurrection on the third day. You can do all things through Christ who gives you strength. Like the Eagle you can rest your head on the pillow of God's Word, for this is what God says to you: "This is the resting place, let the weary rest," and, "this is the place of repose." (Isaiah 28: 12) God has prepared a place of rest for you where you can come in and rest from all your worrie s.

Elevation

The process of being lifted up, raised in rank or status, exalted, being improved morally, intellectually, or culturally, the raising of the spirits.

God placed us in a position of victory in all areas of life, because of the blood that Jesus shed for us. The Bible says we are seated in the heavenly places, far above principalities and powers. As a child of God, He has raised you beyond all limitation in Christ Jesus, so take your place.

Age

The eagle is supposed to attain great age.

The righteous

The Lord promises to satisfy the righteous with long life and good health, and show them His salvation. (Psalms 91: 16)

Eats only fresh food

The Eagle will not eat dead meat unless it is in captivity. It prefers all its food fresh and will go out and hunt fresh food every time it is hungry.

If the eagle accidentally eats something that poison his system, he flies high into a rock and stretches himself out (spread eagle) and lays in the sun until the sun's heat draws all the poison out of his system.

God expect the righteous person to come to him everyday for fresh anointing and strength for the day. Every day we are exposed to junke from the TV, gossip, bitterness, disapointments, anger, and many other things that poison our spirit. We need to be refreshed daily in his presence that's why he says in Isaiah 40: 31 "that those who wait on the Lord, who expect, look for, and hope in Him, shall change and renew their strength and power; they shall lift their wings and mount up close to God as the eagles mount up to the sun; they shall walk and not faint or become tired. We need to come into his presence daily with praise and thanksgiving in our hearts. No matter your age spending time in his presence will renew your life. Lets emulate these powerful attributes from the eagle that makes it such a unique bird amongst all the birds in the world. Let us endeavour to be women who love God and spend quality time in his presence.

The emblem of power

Many nations use the eagle's head on their coat of arms as an emblem of power.

Five thousand years ago the Sumerians of the city-kingdom of Lagash, in the Euphrates Valley, used the "spread-eagle" as the symbol of their power as did Imperial Rome, and as the United States of America does today. The coat of arms of the former Russian and Austrian Empires bore double-headed eagles.

The righteous

Many nations use the eagle for their symbol of power, God is also calling the righteous to take His Word and apply it in all areas of life, to be productive and fruitful, even at a ripe old age. The righteous are created to have dominion and power. They are not created for defeat. All the power in the world is available to a righteous man. That is God's promise for the older woman. You are meant to be a symbol of power to the glory of God.

Let's go into the Bible to meet the second old couple whom God gave a fresh start.

A fresh start

Elizabeth and Zachariah. Walking uprightly

"No good thing does he withhold from those whose walk is blameless." (Psalms 84: 11)

In the time of Herod, king of the Judea, there was a priest named Zachariah who belong to the priestly division of Abijah; his wife, Elizabeth, was also a descendant of Aaron. Both of them were upright in the sight of God, observing all the Lord's commandments and regulations blamelessly, but they had no children because Elizabeth was barren and they were well on in years. (Luke 1: 5-7)

An angel of the Lord appeared to him and said to him "Do not be afraid, Zachariah. Your prayers have been heard, your wife Elizabeth will bear you a son and you are to give him the name John." (Luke 1: 13)

Zachariah asked the angel, "How can I be sure of this? I'm an old man and my wife is well on in years." (Luke 1: 18)

"After this, his wife Elizabeth became pregnant. When it was time for her to have the baby, she gave birth to a son. Her neighbours and relations heard that Lord had shown her great mercy and they shared her joy." (Luke 1: 57-58)

Zachariah questioned the angel of God; he was thinking, reasoning, in his mind how this could be possible, an old man and an old woman having a child. He could not see how it would be possible for them to have a child at their age. Here again we see a man's reasoning and his thoughts trying to hinder his blessing. "How?" he asked the angel of the Almighty God, the more-than-enough God, the God of new beginnings, the God who specialises in impossibilities. Nobody asks God how it can be done because with God all things are possible.

The Bible records that because of his doubt, he was not able to speak until the day God's Word came to pass and the child was born according to the Word of God. Even at a ripe old age, God gave this couple a fresh start, Why? Because they were (people) planted by God's riverside. They were upright and faithful and they were a praying couple and God blessed them because of their commitment to Him.

> Planted in the house of the Lord - they shall flourish in the courts of our God. (Psalms 92: 13)

Planted - what a word! Let us see what the dictionary says:

To plant: to put in the ground, in soil for growth. To set or sow (land) with seed or plants. To plant means to sow or set in the land with seed for growth. When you are planted in the house of God, you become God's own crop, Just like a plant needs water and manure for it to grow, so also you draw your nourishment from the Word of God, and the Holy Spirit feeds you as you draw in the Word of God. The farmer waters the plants. So also the righteous draws water, nourishment, from the river of God.

> Blessed is the man that walketh not in the counsel of the ungodly, nor standeth in the way of sinners, nor sitteth in the seat of the scornful. But his delight is in the law of the Lord; and in his law doth he meditate day and night. And he shall be like a tree planted by the rivers of water, that bringeth forth his fruit in his season; his leaf also shall not wither; and whatsoever he doeth shall prosper. (Psalms 1: 1-3)

Psalm 1 talks of the blessedness of a righteous man. It says, "He is like a tree planted by streams of water, which yields its fruit in season, and whose leaves do not wither. Whatever he does prospers."

A righteous man prospers because his ways are blessed before God. His joy and happiness remain intact, because he delights himself in God's Word. He conforms to its requirements and is the man who is blessed, who is prosperous - he is a happy man.

God is always delighted to ensure the prosperity and the happiness of the righteous. To obey His commands is true wisdom, bringing in the fruitfulness of goodness in all areas of life.

The Word of God discloses to man the way of goodness, and so teaches him the way of happiness.

A tree planted by the riverside

A righteous man is like a tree planted by the riverside - God's riverside.

God's river - the river of life

This is a brief look at the river of God, which is where the righteous man is planted, and where he gets his nourishment daily. No woman drawing nourishment from this river can be barren, no matter her age.

> Then the angel showed me the river of the water of life, as clear as crystal, flowing from the throne of God and of the Lamb (Jesus Christ) down the middle of the great street of the city. On each side of the river stood the tree of life, bearing twelve crops of fruit, yielding its fruit every month. And the leaves of the tree are for the healing of the nations. (Revelation 22: 1-2)

On the river of God, we meet the tree which is where "the righteous receive their full nourishment, whatever they desire. Just as a plant draws water through its roots to nourish all its parts, so a righteous man draws his nourishment from God's river to meet all his daily needs. The fruit of this tree never withers. Its fruit never fails to yield. Every month it produces abundant crops.

So, indeed, as you draw strength from God, through prayer, reading the Bible, praise and worship and fellowship with the Holy Spirit you are supposed to continue to produce fruit, even up to old age - both spiritual and physical fruit. When you are righteous, you live in a world where a lot of things affect the physical circumstance of our lives, but as one who is drawing strength and nourishment from God, through Jesus Christ, you become an evergreen.

Evergreen: A tree or plant which retains its green foliage throughout the year.

The righteous person retains his or her productivity and fruitfulness day in day out, year in year out. That's why Abraham and Sarah had Isaac when Abraham was a 100 years old and Zachariah and Elizabeth had John at a ripe old age, because they were planted at God's riverside.

The Lord one day asked me: "Veronica, why do you think I waited until Sarah was ninety-one years old before I gave her a son?"

I said, "I don't know, Lord." He said, "I wanted it to be an example to every woman below that age that she can have a child at any age because I am the God who created her and gave her my Word; that if she is planted in my house that she will still bear fruit at a ripe old age."

I want to leave you with this, all you beautiful women of God. Jesus loves you and He wants you to know that you can succeed through Christ who gives you strength. God's Word cancels every other report that you have received which contradicts God's plans for your life. If God says "you can" then no human on earth can tell you, "you can't" because with God all things are possible. The only person that can stop you is yourself. If you believe God's Word, and hold on to it as true, then it is bound to be made tangible in your life. You see God's Word can never fail. If He said it, then it is true and not void of power.

God gives life to the dead

The Bible records that, "God gives life to the dead, and calls things that are not as though they were. (Romans 4: 17)

Even though Abraham's and Sarah's reproductive organs were dead, they knew God gives life to the dead. They believed God was able to resurrect every dead organ in their bodies.

Secondly, God calls those things that are "not as though they were". So while we humans tend to look at the limitations, once God gives His Word, He calls those things that "are not as though they were", because His Word cannot return to Him void. It must accomplish what it has been sent to do. (Isaiah 55: 11)

That's why the moment the Word of God is spoken into a situation, those things that "are not must become a reality.

Abraham did not waver through unbelief regarding the promise of God, but was strengthened in his faith and gave glory to God. Being fully persuaded that God had the power to do what He had promised. (Romans 4: 20-21)

The Bible says:

> If the spirit of God who raised Jesus from the dead is living in you, he who raised Jesus from the dead will also give life to your mortal bodies through his spirit who lives in you. (Romans 8: 11)

This scripture is so important for the woman who has been told all her eggs have passed their usefulness. The Bible says in Romans 4: 17, "that God gives life to the dead and calls things that are not as though they were" - because this is how God gives life to things that are not, by calling them forth. You are going to use the power of your words to call back every dead or non-existent part of your reproductive organs so that it will function the way God intended, because you are a righteous woman.

For each medical problem we mention, we are going to add the Word of God on how to deal with it, as we continue to deal with how to help the older woman conceive. The Bible prayers are daily confessions which you should confess until there is full manifestation of all you want from the Lord.

Womb

In old age the womb gets smaller and in old age may be quite tiny. The ligaments and tissues surrounding and supporting the uterus may become weakened, and result in a prolapse of one form or another.

Prolapse

This simply means slipping forward or downwards. Where the uterus is concerned, there are varying degrees of this 'slipping' or dropping downwards, the greatest being a complete prolapse, where the uterus appears right outside the vagina. Other minor types of prolapse may occur with or without much involvement of the uterus.

The Bible

The Bible tells us that even though the womb has shrunk and is weak, using the power of your words as we discussed in the chapter on the power of God's Word, and your own words, you should pray this prayer:

"Father, in the name of Jesus, I apply your Word to my womb. The Bible says your Word is alive, full of life. I speak life back into my womb, in the Name of Jesus. Your Word can **energise,** I speak to my womb, or any part of it that has suffered a prolapse, to become energised and alive in obedience to Your Word. I command that the right e nvironment be created by Your Word to sustain the life of the children you have given me from the fondations of the earth. I thank you father, for it is done in Jesus' name." Father, remember your promise to me that I your daughter will be like a fruitful vine within my home. (Psalm 128:3) I thank you beacause that's what I am in Jesus name. Amen.

The ovaries

We have discussed earlier on the function of the ovaries, where the ovaries are now empty of ova (eggs) It then becomes imposs ible for the older woman to conceive. You speak the Word of God to your ovaries in Jesus' name.

The Bible

"Father, in the name of Jesus Christ, I speak your Word into my ovaries. The Bible says your Word is **effective**. I say to my ovaries become effective in the mighty name of Jesus. I command that my ovaries be put in full operation, by the powerful Word of God which energises. I thank God that my ovaries is now performing all the normal functions that have stopped, in Jesus' name."

Ovulation

In the first part of a woman's normal menstrual cycle, (average cycle for most women is twenty-one - twenty-eight days) mainly FSH is produced, with a small amount of LH. FSH has an effect on the ovaries, stimulating the "follicles" containing the eggs to ripen, and several of these stimulated follicles come to the surface of the ovary. One of these ripened follicles reaches the surface first, and the surrounding follicle wall, now quite thin, ruptures and releases the eggs or ovum; ovulation has taken place.

But for the older women, this does not happen any more. So based upon the Word of God, speak to your body for ovulation to take place.

The Bible

Father, in the name of Jesus Christ, I speak your Word to my body. Your Word is **powerful**. It has great influence. In Jesus' Name I command that FSH and LH be produced to stimulate my ovaries. I ask that your powerful Word penetrate and influence my ovulation to become **effective** in the Name of Jesus.

The Vagina

Thinning of the vaginal skin may also occur, but again, this is usually minimal in the early pre-menopausal years. With age the vaginal skin takes on a typically inflamed appearance, reddened, thin, with tiny spots of haemorrhage under the skin. Dryness during sexual intercourse may occur. Vaginal soreness may also be a factor. The vulva may become thin, and shrinkage of the opening of the vagina may occur.

The Bible

Sarah had pleasure at ninety years of age, if you are younger than her, there is no reason why you should not have pleasure also.

Based on the Word of God which is *"energising"*, I say that my vagina is energised, in Jesus' name, facilitating it to function normally as God intended it to. I ask, in Jesus' Name, that the Word of God become **operative**, exacting power and influence against factors operating against joy and love in my marriage, and I command the operative power of God's Word to bring about and cause my vagina to function as God intended it, in Jesus' name. Amen.

The Breasts

With the stoppage of the production of cyclical hormone stimulus to the breasts, it is not surprising that the breasts become less firm, diminish in size and the nipples, too, become smaller and flatter.

The Bible

I decided to add this, because a woman's breasts are so important. Mother needs full, lively breasts, not only for daddy, but for baby. In the Bible, Sarah was ninety-one years old and yet the Bible records what she said, "Who would have said to Abraham that Sarah would nurse children at the breast?" (Genesis 21: 7) We see a ninety-one year old mother nursing on the breast. What did God do here? His Word became **alive** - making her breast become vigorous, active, performing the right action; making milk. God's Word also became **energising** - it revived her dead breast, giving it energy, to facilitate normal operation - production of milk.

Confession

Based on the Word of God which is active I command in the name of Jesus that my breasts come alive and become vigorous and active, to perform the right action. I ask the Word of God to energise my breast to produce milk for my baby in the name of Jesus.

I have written all of God's promises for you beautiful women of God; grow these promises in your heart and they will bear fruit in Jesus' name.

The Bible says, "our dead will live; their dead bodies will rise. You who dwell in the dust, wake up and shout for joy. Your dew is like the dew of the morning. (Isaiah 26: 19) I want to encourage you, God's beautiful women, don't doubt God's Word. He alone can and is able to give life back to anything that is dead in your life. He calls those things that "are not as though they were". That's God's way of seeing things. You may look and see nothing, but if you look through God's eyes, you will see your body working effectively as God wants it.

Hold on to these promises, God is faithful and able. Once again I leave you with God's promises to you.

The Bible says that,

> "If the Spirit of God who raised Jesus from the dead is living in you, he who raised Jesus from the dead will also give life to your mortal bodies through his Spirit who lives in you. (Romans 8: 11)

> The righteous will flourish like a palm tree. They will grow like a cedar of Lebanon planted in the house of the Lord; they will flourish in the courts of our God; *they will still bear fruit in old age; they will stay fresh and green* proclaiming, the Lord is upright, he is my rock and there is no wickedness in him. (Psalms 92: 12-15)

Can you better the Word of God? You see, His promise is clear. A woman who trusts in Him can still bear fruit - have children in old age, stay fresh and green - which means your reproductive organs are meant to remain healthy and productive, because you are drawing life from God.

Chapter Twelve

Questions an older woman may ask

Q1: Question - will my baby be born with a genetic disorder, because of my age?

I know many women who want to have a baby will be afraid and say, "What if my baby is born with a genetic disorder because of my age?" I really want to address this issue from the Word of God. In the first instance we saw that Elizabeth and Zachariah had John the Baptist at a great age, and that child was born perfect. We see Abraham and Sarah had Isaac at 100 years but he was a perfect child. God blessed this older couple with perfect children. The Bible says every good and perfect gift comes from God. (James 1: 17) God will not bless you with the gift of a deformed child if you ask Him for a child. You may say, "Well, Elizabeth and Sarah were different." No! The Bible says God shows no favouritism. What he did for one He will do for the other if you can find it in His Word. God is true and faithful and He is merciful and just. Do not be afraid to ask God for what you want; God wants to bless you with a perfect baby who will bring joy and happiness into your life. God bless you.

Q2: I am an older woman and I am not married and I desire to have children. What does God have for me?

The Bible says that at your age - the age at which you are now and also the situation in which you are now - God will satisfy your desire. (Psalms 103: 5) This scripture is quite clear. If you desire is to be happily married and have children at the age you are now, then God promises to satisfy that desire. Our Lord Jesus Christ said to us "ask and you will receive", so all you need to do is ask. Ask God to bless you with one of His wonderful sons who you can spend the rest of your family life with. God Himself said, "It is not good for man (woman) to be alone." Man did not say this, God Himself said it because He is the one who created us all and knows our basic needs. God Himself said that if you ask Him for bread, He will not give you a stone.

110

Today I want to encourage you to ask God to bless you with a home and a husband and children and if your heart's desire is sincere I know God will do it for you.

Remember this biblical promise: "No good thing will be withheld from those who love Him." Ask in faith and trust Him to be faithful to bless you.

Q3: *Because of my age, will I die while my children are still young?*

Many people are against older women having children because they say the woman will die and leave very young children without a mother. I personally believe that this is wrong. Death has not and has never had anything to do with age. We have seen very young people die without fulfilling their destiny and leaving young children behind. Life is something that is given to everyone and the choice of how we live it is left to us individuals. I want the older woman to hear this today. You will not die before your child or children are grown up, for this is God's promise to you. *"With long life will I satisfy you and show you my salvation."* (Psalm 92:16) *You will still bear fruit in old age. You will stay fresh and green.* (Psalm 94.14) From these Bible promises we get an idea of what God has for the older woman. He wants you to live to full old age and see your children's children. Forget what fear is saying and start listening to what God is saying to you today. Take His Word and let it bless you so that your life and your joy is full. For the Bible says, a child born in old age will do this for you: *will renew your life and sustain you in your old age.* (Ruth 4:15)

Chapter Thirteen

The Power Of God's Word - And The Power Of You Own Words

One of the attributes of God's Word is it's infallibility. The Bible says Heaven and earth will pass away but not a *tittle* of God's Word will fail. God said the "words that come out of His mouth will not return to Him void, but accomplish the purpose for which they are sent," (Isaiah 55: 11) - which means God's words will never return to him empty. No! They will always accomplish their purpose and that is why I advise you today, that if you agree with any biblical promise you read in this book as the Word of God, and you apply it in your situation, it will surely accomplish that which it is meant to accomplish.

The Word of God is alive

Jesus said that "the words which I speak to you are both spirit and life." That means every Word of God is already power-packed, carrying with it the power to manifest itself. God does not need your help or mine to let His words be fulfilled. All He requires from us is to trust (have faith) that what He has said He is able to bring to pass. Obedience is also important on your part. God may ask you to do things which may look or seem stupid to the ordinary man but obedience will lead you to inherit God's promises. Isaiah 55: 8-9- says that "God's way is not man's way and God's thoughts are not man's thoughts - His ways are higher than our ways and His thoughts higher than our thoughts." You can boldly say to yourself that because God's Word carries miracle working power, the fulfilment of your need is not in you but it is in God's promise to you.

The Word of God creates

The Word of God does not only heal but it can create whatever

112

parts of the body you may be missing or needing. Read in John 1: 14 - "The word became flesh." This is so important for those needing creative miracles. The very word you have received concerning your need can be converted so that it becomes flesh - this work will be done in your spirit and the manifestation will appear in the physical as a creative miracle, in the area of your need. For example, in Genesis 1: 3, God wanted light and said, "Let there be light," and there was light. The Word God spoke quickly turned into flesh and manifested itself into light. Let's take, for example, the possibility that you need a new vagina or womb. You can call it into flesh by the Word of God spoken out of your own mouth and it will become flesh - tangible in your life.

> For God said from now on I tell you of new things, of hidden things unknown to you. They are created now and not long ago; you have not heard of them before today. (Isaiah 48: 6-7)

From this you can clearly see that God is still creating new things because he is able to create.

The Word of God sanctifies you

Our Lord Jesus Christ prayed this prayer for us -Sanctify them by the truth; your word is truth. (John 17: 17) What does the word "sanctify" mean? it means to be set apart for a special purpose or sacred (Holy) purpose.

Every woman is set apart by God for a special purpose as a precious vessel through which God can bring a child into the world. Why? Because childbirth is special and holy to God.

God watches over his Word to see that it is performed: (Jeremiah 1:12)

What is to watch? it means to keep guard, to keep awake during the night especially to keep vigil, to be closely observant of an event or action, to watch while alert or to guard or to protect closely; that's what God does over His words. He hovers over them like a mother hen hovers over her chicks. He who watches over *Israel* (you and me) will neither slumber or sleep. (Psalm 121: 4) Can you imagine that your God does not sleep but that he is watching over all the words he has spoken to you until they are performed? His words can be totally trusted and depended on.

The Word of God sustains everything on earth

"The Son is the radiance of God's glory, and the exact representation of His being, sustaining all things by His powerful Word." (Hebrews 1: 3) We can see clearly that the Word of God is what is ruling the world today. God created this world with His Word and is still sustaining and running everything with it. You and I, and everybody in the world is subject to God's Word and everything, including infertility, and all human problems must bow to the Word of God.

The Word of God is the remedy for impossible situations

The Word of God can be used in all situations. Because of its infallibility it is the only remedy for impossible situations in the world today. "For what is impossible with man is possible with God." (Luke 1: 37)

THE POWER OF YOUR WORD

Having discussed the power of God's words, now I would also like us to go into the Word of God to see what God has said about our words. I also want you to know that the greatest battle you will ever face is not infertility. The greatest battle you have to fight is getting your words in line with God's Word, to bring about your miracle.

Everyone, created by God, has the ability to express themselves, their plans, thoughts, perceptions, heart's desires, and visions, through words. God has given us the ability to express our innermost desires through words.

Why?

This is what the Holy Spirit taught me.

The Lord God formed the man from the *dust of the ground,* and breathed into his nostrils the breath of life, and the man became a living being. (Genesis 2:7)

God created man from the dust as the Bible says, but how many of us know that nothing can be created with fine dry particles of solid matter? What is dust? The dictionary says that 'dust is fine, dry particles of any solid matter, especially earth'. They are particles which the body disintegrates or decays into. God needed some form of liquid to turn

114

that dusty sand into something soft, that could be moulded and shaped. That's where His saliva came into play. God applied His saliva to that sand, and it became a soft, sticky mixture of mud or clay, which could be shaped or moulded.

The human saliva is medically proven to contain a mixture of water, protein, salt and enzyme, that is secreted into the mouth by glands that lubricate ingested food, and it often begins the break-down of starches. I believe God's saliva not only contains what ours contains, but it also contains life-giving power. Our Lord Jesus Christ said, "The words that I speak to you, they are spirit and life." (John 6: 63)

Have you ever wondered why Jesus spat on the ground, made some mud with the saliva and put it on the eyes of the man born blind? (John 9: 6)

God's saliva gave life to the human flesh

The saliva came from God's mouth. It gave life to the flesh, because it contained life in it. Then when God breathed into the man's nostrils with His mouth again, the life in the saliva ignited together with the life in His breath, and the man became a living being.

God programmed your body to respond to His Word

Now, this is the interesting part. God programmed every part of man to respond to His Word. Because His saliva is in every part of our bodies, therefore, every part of our bodies must respond to the Word of God. Our bodies actually hear, understand and obey God's Word, because the Creator programmed each part with His saliva in order to give life to it.

When the body hears the Word of God, it responds and obeys it, because God has programmed it that way. The Bible says (in Proverbs 18: 21), "The power of life and death is in the tongue." Have you ever really thought about these words? God has put the power that holds your life in your mouth. If you are to succeed or fail in life, it is going to be up to you. You hold the power in your tongue to build your life, either for death or for life. It is up to you.

You can programme yourself by the Word of God. When you feel as though you are falling sick, instead of accepting it, you can say to yourself, "What does the Bible say about this?" It says, "By His stripes I am healed." (Isaiah 53: 5) If it looks like that baby is not going to come you can look at what the Word of God says: "In Christ I will bear much fruit." Therefore you don't say what the circumstance is saying. You say what God says. Your body hears and sooner or later it will line up with the Word of the Manufacturer Who programmed it to work and run perfectly on His Word. What will happen to a car if you fill the tank up with water? That is exactly what many of us have done to our bodies. God has left us the manual (Holy Bible), telling us the Manufacturer's instructions for use and the remedies in case of emergency, but all we have done is ignore it, and run up and down looking for help where we can't find it.

The Bible says:

> The mouth of a righteous man is a well of life. (Proverbs 10: 11)

> The mouth of the just bringeth forth wisdom, but the forward tongue shall be cut out. The lips of the righteous know what is acceptable. (Proverbs 10:31-32)

A righteous man is supposed to know what is acceptable. In our speech, what God said is what is acceptable. When you begin to quote what God said, it will just be as though God said it Himself. It will work for you like it worked for Him. If you programme your spirit with God's Word, and do not doubt in your heart, but believe that those things which you are saying will come to pass, they will come to pass.

Do you believe that the baby will be born? Do you believe that missing chromosomes can be re-created? Do you believe that sexual organs can be re-created? If you believe, start to say it now. Our Lord Jesus Christ made this statement about our speech.

> I tell you the truth, If anyone says to this mountain, Go throw yourself into the sea, and does not doubt what he says, it will be done for him. (Mark 11: 22)

This is a fact. It is the law of the Spirit. It can never fail, because it is the Word of God. This statement speaks for itself. If you face anything which is lacking, which has caused infertility in your life, by saying what the Word of God says, you can turn it around. Jesus Himself said that you can have what you ask for, whether good or bad.

Whatever miracle you desire today, you must confess it from your mouth. It may not manifest itself today or tomorrow or next week, or next month, but if what you are saying lines up with the Word of God, it must surely come to pass. At times it may look like there is no change. It may look like nothing is happening. It may look like God is not hearing you, but I can say today, if you stand on God's Word, it will surely come to pass.

When you confess it, some may laugh at you. Others will think you are stupid, but please don't listen to anyone. Keep your focus on God and His Word.

Jesus Christ is the High Priest of our confession (Hebrews 3: 1)

Christianity itself, is a confession. When you confess, you confess with your lips. What do we confess? We confess the "finished work of Christ for us." We confess that He is seated at the right hand of the Father, having redeemed us from the penalty of sin. We confess that He has, "Blessed us with every spiritual blessing in the Heavenly Realms in Christ. (Ephesians 1: 3) We confess that we are healed already. These are the things you are to confess. God has promised us this:

> Peace, peace to him who is far off and to him who is near! says the Lord, I create the fruit of his lips and I will heal him (make his lips blossom anew with speech in thankful praise. (Isaiah 57: 19)

God has promised that He will create the fruit of your lips. So what do you want created? Make sure that is what you are confessing or saying from your mouth. And God will bring it to pass.

In concluding this chapter, this is my advice to you. Please don't go around telling people all your troubles to get their sympathy. It will not help you. Cast all your cares on the Lord, because He cares for you.

Telling people all your problems, only makes you lose faith with God, and puts you in doubt. But saying what God's Word says, in spite of every circumstance, brings faith into your heart. The living Word of God on your lip makes you a victor, makes infertility and disease your servant - it brings God on the scene - brings victory and joy and success.

Example of a person who did not watch his words: Luke 1

> Zachariah and his wife had prayed for years to have a child. Finally God sent an Angel to tell him his wife was going to

117

conceive and have a son. When the Angel told him his wife was going to have a child, Zachariah asked the Angel, "How can I be sure of this? I am an old man and my wife is well on in years..."

The Angel answered, "I am Gabriel, I stand in the presence of God, and I have been sent to speak to you and to tell you this good news. And now you will be silent and not able to speak until the day this happens, because you did not believe my words, which will come true at their proper time."

Meanwhile, the people were waiting for Zachariah and wondering why he stayed so long in the temple. When he came out, he could not speak to them. They realised he had seen a vision in the temple, for he kept making signs to them, but remained unable to speak. (Luke 1: 18-22)

Here we see God take an extreme action to shut a man up, for the Bible records that throughout Elizabeth's pregnancy, Zachariah was unable to speak.

On the eighth day, after the child was born, they came to circumcise the child, and they were going to name him after his father, Zachariah, but his mother spoke up.

Then they made signs to Zachariah to find out what he would like to name the child. He asked for a writing tablet, and to everyone's astonishment he wrote, "His name is John. Immediately his mouth was opened and his tongue was loosed." (Luke 1: 59-64)

Here God bound Zachariah's tongue so that his prayers might be fulfilled and that the favour of the Lord might be upon Elizabeth, as God had spoken. As soon as this came to pass, God loosed his tongue. I am sure God took this extreme measure because Zachariah could have killed this miracle with his mouth, because the Bible says the power of life and death are in our tongue. And the child born was so important in the plan of God for the world. Many of you carry seeds of great destiny, so watch your words in order that God's favour may rest on you and your family. Remember, the power of life and death are in your tongue.

Chapter Fourteen

The Power Of Praise And Worship

In this chapter we will be dealing with the importance of Praise and Worship in receiving your blessings from God.

What is praise and worship?

Praise means to glorify or extol God, to magnify God and bless him. To worship is to honour or reverence as a divine being or supernatural power, to regard with great, even extra respect, honour or devotion, to perform or take part in an act of worship to God.

God dwells in our praise

The Bible tells us that God inhabits the praises of His people. (Psalms 22: 3) What does the word inhabit mean? It means, God lives in, dwells in, manifest himself in "the praises of His people. When we praise God, we have the Lord as a boarder, an in-dweller in us.

For many of you today who face difficult situations or seemingly impossible situations, what you need to do is praise God. When you want God to inhabit your midst, your circumstances, your difficulties you can do nothing better than to praise Him, for when you praise him you are assured of His abiding presence inhabiting every life situation that may confront you. Today I want you to get one thing clear; the only thing you and I can ever offer to God is our praise. We cannot give him money, there is nothing we can give him except praise.

The Bible commands all to praise the Lord. It says that if we don't praise Him, the stones will cry out. God is worthy to be praised. The moon, the stars and even the beautiful flowers praise Him. All mountains and hills break out into praise before the God of all the earth.

How wonderful it is that God says in Psalms 50: 23 "that he who sacrifices thank-offerings honours me and he prepares the way so that I may show him the salvation of God." So you see when you start to offer God a sacrifice of praise these are some of the benefits available to you.

Benefits of praise

* Praise unlocks the windows of Heaven.
* Praise causes doubt to flee.
* Praise brings down showers of blessings.
* Praise brings down the love and peace of God.
* Praise brings freedom from bondage.
* Praise changes every situation.
* Praise establishes your heart in God and brings God into the circumstances.
* Praise is the master key to God's store house.

When you become established in praise you become a *true worshipper of God* - and you thus prepare your way to reap God's blessings.

In writing on praise today, I would like to take you back to some of the testimonies of the people we used from the Bible in this book. We will be discussing David and King Jehosphat and I will also be sharing my personal experience of praise with you. May the Holy Spirit quicken your understanding and help you understand the truth of the power of praise and run with it in Jesus' name.

David

In the solution to the low sperm count in my men's book I used the story of David and Goliath. We see in the life of David a beautiful example of God's hand of protection overshadowing him, preserving him from destruction. In his youth David was attacked by lions and bears and later he encountered a giant Goliath on the field of battle. Against all these overwhelming odds, David was not killed but rather he destroyed those bent on destroying him.

What was David's secret?

All his confidence and trust was in the Lord. His boasting was not of any man, but it was of the Lord. David said to Goliath, "You come against me with swords and spear and javelin, but I come against you in the name of the Lord Almighty". (I Samuel 17: 45)

David said, "All those gathered here will know that it is not by sword or spear that the Lord saves, for the battle is the Lord's and he will give all of you into our hands." (I Samuel 17: 47) For many of you facing infertility today, learn from David; his boasting and confidence was not of what any human could do, it was based on what God could do for him. David lived a life of praise; throughout the Bible are Psalms of praise, written by David to God. In Psalms 34: 1, he declared: "I will bless the Lord at all times, his praise shall continually be in my mouth."

This was his secret; God's praise was continually on his lips. David knew the power of praise for he also declared that: "God inhabits the praises of his people." He knew God dwelt in our praises and nothing could stop him praising God. David listed some of God's benefits to him for his life of praise as:

* redemption from destruction
* forgiveness for all our sins
* healing of all diseases (Psalms 103: 2-4)

David recounted these benefits and attributed them to his continued praise to his God.

David discovered that when we praise God He inhabits the praise, manifests Himself in our praise. With God constantly "on the scene", in response to our praise, we are protected by God himself.

My personal experience of praise

To me praise is where I live; day and night the praise of God never ceases from my lips. If you were to spend a day in my home you would be totally infected by the Spirit of praise - on my life. Many people come into my home and plan to spend an hour and end up staying two to three hours, unable to move. They will make comments like, "There is so much peace in your home, Sister Vero." Why is it so? Because of Praise. I praise God everywhere, I praise, I dance; my children have now adopted this too for they also dance to the Lord. The praise of God has never ceased upon my lips because God has been so faithful to me and my family.

Some of the benefits of praise that I have received

Praise releases Faith. There have been times I have faced impossible situations in my life, but because of praise, my attention has been drawn away from the situation to focusing on God, who causes all things to work together for our good and to His glory.

Bailiffs sent away

Because of the power of praise, bailiffs have been prevented from repossessing our home on three occasions. The second time they came, I just sat in my home praising God and the bailiffs went and hid in a corner near my house. They could not come near our home. All this I can testify to the glory of God - that it is the power of praise.

Praise draws me nearer to God

My love and relationship with God has been founded and established on praise. I have so found myself drawn nearer and nearer to Him as I worship Him and praise Him that His character rubs off on me from day to day. His praise has continually been on my lips. I praise him all the time; this book you are reading was born through praise. Even when it looked like it would never be written, I just lifted up my eyes to Him and praised Him, for He who gave the call is able to accomplish. Whatever you need in life, praise and trust in God and He will bring it to pass in your life.

King Jehoshaphat

In idiopathic infertility we used King Jehoshaphat as an example of what we are to do when we face impossible situations. King Jehoshaphat faced three enemy armies fully armed for battle against his kingdom.

What did he do? He armed his people with praise to God. He appointed singers to sing to the Lord, praising the beauty of God's holiness, as they went out before the army. They were to sing "praise the Lord, for His mercy endures forever." When they began to sing and praise, "the Lord set an ambush against the children of Ammon, Moab and Mount Seir, which were come against Judah and they were smitten." (2 Chronicles 20: 19-22)

This is how God fights our battles when we praise him. As we praise God, He finishes off the rest of the battle Himself. All the battles that we face in our lives belong to the Lord for He fights for us in the midst of our praise. The Bible says:

> It is good to praise the Lord and make music to your name,
> O Most High, to proclaim your love in the morning and your

faithfulness at night, to the music of ten-stringed lyre and the melody of harp. For you make me glad by your deeds O Lord...how profound is your thoughts!" (Psalms 92: 1-5)

When you start to proclaim your love to God, telling him how great and mighty he is, proclaiming His faithfulness in the morning and at night, God starts to bring victory into your life. Praise is the Christian's gun of battle; when the battles of life rage hard, the Christian who is fully armed with praise is well clothed for battle. God has commanded us to give him praise at all times, and for His praise to be continually on our lips. When God's praise is continually on your lips you cannot be defeated.

Today I encourage all the couples who face impossible situations to lift up their voices in praise of God. As you do that the peace and glory of God will come upon you. You say that you don't know how to praise God.

The Psalms are full of praise songs. Psalms like Psalm 100, 159, 150, 117, You can use those psalms to praise God. When I started my walk with God, all I knew was "glory to God" and I used to repeat that over and over again and the glory of God used to hit me so hard so that I could hardly move. So praise him any way you know. The important thing is the heart of the person who is praising; as you praise Him, His blessing flows into your life.

Chapter Fifteen

Giving

Today, in writing about giving, I would like to introduce you to the greatest giver of all. He is God Almighty. The Bible says that, "God so loved the world that He gave His only begotten Son." (John 3:16)

Have you ever imagined what it cost God to give His only Son to redeem the world from death? I guess this is one thing we all can never understand. At times when I talk to people about the death of Christ, they just ask questions like, "Was it necessary for Him to die for us? Why did God not just kill Satan instead?" These questions are good questions, but the truth of all this is this; if it was not necessary God would never have crucified His Son.

Today in the body of Christ, giving has become a controversial subject. Many people don't like talking about it; they have their own ideas about giving which has nothing to do with Christ. The people that complain are the same as those who will go to a fertility clinic and pay thousands of pounds for a treatment that may never succeed. If you did not pay that money the fertility clinic will have to shut down their business for lack of money; this is the same with the gospel of Jesus Christ. The Word of God is free, but those who preach the gospel need finance as well to pay church bills, electricity bills, etc. What will you say if you got to church on a winter's morning and there is no heating because the bills have not been paid? If you are sitting in a cold church you will not be able to hear the Word of God properly. So for the effective preaching of God's Word we must learn to give.

Personally, this book will not be complete without my advising and telling you the truth about giving.

If you read through the Bible you will discover that our God is a God who loves to give and we as his children must also learn to give. I am not saying God will not bless you because you did not give. But there are certain levels of blessings attached to giving. Let us look at the the giving of :-

Manoah and his wife

The first couple we are going to be talking about is Manoah and his wife. In Judges 13 is the Bible account of Manoah and his wife who were sterile: barren. The angel of the Lord came to this couple and told them they were going to conceive and have a son. After the angel gave them instructions on what to do, then

> Manoah said to the Angel of the Lord, "We would like you to stay until we prepare a young goat for you." The Angel of the Lord replied, "Even though you detain me, I will not eat any of your food. But if you prepare a burnt offering, offer it to the Lord. (Judges 13: 15-16)

This couple not only loved God, they knew how to worship God. They would not let the angel of God go without giving God what they could afford. Notice that God did not ask for this offering, but this couple decided to offer it.

When they offered this sacrifice, as he and his wife watched, the flame blazed up from the sacrifice towards Heaven, "the angel of the Lord ascended in the flame." (Judges 13: 20)

God accepted this offering of thanks. It was pleasing to Him and that sealed their blessing.

My personal experience of giving

I also want to share my testimony on giving to encourage you to give to build the body of Christ. For the Gospel of Jesus Christ to spread all over the world, it is going to need those who are committed to sacrificial giving.

The first day I gave my heart to the Lord, the Lord lead me to buy three books that totally changed my life, and laid a foundation for my Christian walk. One of these books was *Dream Seed* by Mike Murdock.

In this book I learnt some of the most powerful principles of giving in my life. The very next Sunday, when I was going to church, I went to the bank and took out some money I had saved. I put that money in an envelope and dropped it in the offering basket, to be used for the work of God.

After that Service, we went to a brother's house with his family and my friends. While there we were praying and that was when God came to me and made me this promise. He said to me, *"Veronica, because of that offering you gave today, the blessing I have for you will flow like the widow's oil. You will not have room to store it.* (2 Kings 4)

I started weeping with joy, because I was happy that my offering was acceptable to God. Up to this time of my writing, I have not yet stepped into the widow's oil blessing physically, but I believe that spiritually I have stepped in there. because I feel it stirring up in my spirit. Seven years down the road, I can boldly write and say, I have sought the kingdom of God with all my heart. Everything I could give to build the body of Christ, I have given. God has also been faithful to me. Not once has He withheld any good thing from me. His blessings have remained upon my life. Every penny I have, I have sowed into God's work. I will not bother to write about the sacrifices that I have made in order to be able to continue to give to the body of Christ. This is personally between me and God. But I can boldly say that I have been faithful to God; be it in tithe or offering, God has always been first. I also believe God will bring His promise to pass, because He is a faithful God.

Many of you reading this book may be needing great things that you want God to do for you. I can boldly tell you, when you give, you honour God. You show Him that you care. Each time you open your hand and give to the Glory of God some-thing leaves God's hand to bless you.

Anyone who loves gives. God loved us, He gave His only Son. God keeps giving. No one can out-give God. Please get this clear in your spirit; everything you have comes from God, but God still desires that we take a part of what He has given us to worship Him. Whatever you give is used to build up others less privileged than you. It is used to bless the poor or preach the Gospel.

What you give is not directly given to God in the sense that He has a need. *No!* God has no need. For the whole world, and everything in it belongs to Him, including you and me.

But He has laid down the principle of sowing and reaping and giving and receiving as tools He uses physically to bring blessing into our life.

Have you ever wondered how a farmer sows a handful of seeds

and in a few months reaps a harvest which is greater than the handful of seed he sowed? So it is with sowing into the work of God. Your handful sown will return in a great abundance of harvest, for the Bible says, "whatever a man sows he will reap." (Galatians 5: 7)

You may make a vow like the next person we are going to be looking at.

Hannah

Hannah was a great lady who loved God. She had prayed for years to have a baby. Finally, she got desperate for:

> In bitterness of soul Hannah wept much and prayed to the Lord. And she made a vow, saying "O Lord Almighty, if you will only look upon your servant's misery and remember me, and not forget your servant but give her a son, then I will give him to the Lord for all the days of his life. (I Samuel 1: 10-11)

Here we read of a desperate woman, who wanted a child. She had prayed for years without result. Finally, she decided to give back to God that which she desired most.

The Bible says that in the course of time, God remembered her. "She conceived and gave birth to a son. She named him Samuel, saying, 'Because I asked the Lord for him'" (I Samuel 1: 20).

True to her vows

She was true to her word. For when the boy was weaned, "she took the boy with her, young as he was, along with a three year old bull, an ephah of flour and a skin of wine, and brought him to the house of the Lord at Shiloh." When they slaughtered the bull, they brought the boy to Eli and she said to him:

> "As surely as you live, my lord, I am the woman who stood here beside you praying to the Lord. I prayed for this child and the Lord has granted me what I asked of him. So now I give him to the Lord. For his whole life he shall be given over to the Lord." And she worshipped the Lord. (I Samuel 1: 24-28)

This is the story of a faithful woman. God knew He could trust her.

She proved herself to be faithful to Him. Even giving her son was not enough. When she went to give that son, she brought more offerings to give in the house of God. In those days, nobody could stop her giving. She gave her best to the One Who gave her what nobody could give her.

As I told you earlier, nobody can out-give God. Let us see some of the rewards of this faithful act of this faithful woman.

> Then the Lord was gracious to Hannah; she conceived and gave birth to three sons and two daughters. (I Samuel 2: 21)

We see God's faithfulness demonstrated. He blessed her with two daughters and three more sons, plus Samuel, making Hannah a mother of six children. What a mighty God we serve!

Today, for those of you who desire God's blessing, I encourage you to give whatever you can, but remember this, your gift must be valuable to you. What does not move you will not move God.

This woman gave her best. You too must decide to give your best. No matter what it is, let it be your best.

When I asked God for a son in 1994, I gave him back to God even before I conceived. I told the Lord to give me a son, who will be a man of prayer in His kingdom when he grows up. Today, to the glory of God, my son is almost five years old now, but nobody can stop him praying. He is always praying. So you see, if you are faithful, God will be faithful. Even when you are unfaithful, God remains faithful.

Today, you must make a decision to give. Many pressing needs will be staring you in the face, but you must choose for yourself what to do.

I personally cannot even put a figure to the amount I have sown into God's work in the past few years, but I can boldly say, I have given all that I could without holding back. Hannah gave her son back to God with more offerings on top of that. She gave her best. What will you choose to do today?

You may never know what your giving will accomplish, but give anyway. Forget the critics - those who will not give and love to discourage others from giving. Obey God and see what God will do for you.

Where do I give?

Where you sow your money matters a lot. Let us take, for example, a vineyard owner must plant his vine on a suitable and well drained hill to be able to have a grape harvest. Grapes will not grow on just any ground, so also it is with your giving. I would advise you to give to your church, if you go to church. If not, I would suggest that you ask the Lord to direct you to a good - cause or a ministry of his choice, and then send whatever you desire to give to that ministry. God will bless you as you do that. Even if you don't give, God will still bless you when you believe His Word.

Points of action

- Be specific and ask God what you desire.
- Believe by faith that you have received it.
- Determine in your heart what you want to give to God. Make sure it moves you.
- Be faithful to fulfil it.
- Look for a good soil to sow your seed.
- Keep praising God; at the right time your seed will bear fruit. God bless you.

Chapter Sixteen

Major Questions On Infertility Answered From The Bible

Question: What are the spiritual causes of infertility?

I noticed whilst researching for this book that, medically, little is known about infertility. This got me questioning the Holy Spirit about it. He taught me quite a few things which I have added in this book. Why did I desire to do this? As you read through the pages of this book you will notice it is full of miracles and restoration, but at the same time I must present to you a balanced Gospel. The Gospel of Jesus Christ is balanced; His promises to His Children are many and all are victorious but on the journey to victory are also warnings of great afflictions. "Many are the afflictions of the righteous but the Lord delivers him out of them all." (Psalms 34: 19)

Jesus told us about all the good things that he had in store for us, but he also painted a total picture to prepare us for every situation in life.

There are many reasons scattered throughout the pages of the Bibles as to why infertility happens to many people even among born-again Christians. This is because someone could be born again and still operate under a curse. "Infertility is a curse of the law."In Deuteronomy 28: 15-18 the bible tells us "If you do not obey the Lord your God and do not carefully follow all his commands...all these curses will come upon you...the fruit of your womb will be cursed," as the price of sin and disobedience.When we talk of the curse it is still well worth remembering what Galatians 3: 13-14 says that "Christ has redeemed us from the curse of the law by becoming a curse for us, so that the blessings given to Abraham might come to the Gentiles through Christ Jesus and by faith."

If you, as a child of God, desire to be free from infertility you must take a stand. If there are areas you need to deal with in your life deal with them and then take a stand. Having children is God's greatest desire for man. Procreation is of God, it is God's main reason for creating us.

Imagine if all people on earth, especially Christians, were barren, soon we would have ended up without witnesses. God blesses us with our own children who will spread the Gospel and bring God's love to the world from that family after their ancestors have died. That is why the Bible says that "a good man will always leave an inheritance to His children's children." (Proverbs 13: 22) Why? Because that is God's greatest desire. God alone dreamt up child birth and then created us with that desire in us. The Bible says that God himself desires Godly offspring. (Malachi 2: 15)

Before infertility is experienced in the physical it has already started in the spiritual realm which you and I cannot see into. All of life's battles are won or lost there. Then we experience victory or loss here on earth. Nothing written here is to judge anyone, but it is written so that if anyone finds themselves caught up in any of these situations, there could be a turning around and forsaking of those things so that God's blessings can rest upon you. There is no point praying for a child and then not dealing with the issues that could have led to lack of conception.

May the Holy Spirit help you to grasp the truth and may the revelation knowldgle in this book bring you love, peace and joy in Jesus' name. Amen.

God shuts the womb

At times God himself shuts the womb, waiting for a specific time to bring a special child into the world. The Bible says in Acts 17: 26- that God himself determines the times set for every human being to be born and the exact place where they should live. Even down to parents, location of place of birth, God alone determines it all. The Bible says that there is "a time to be born." (Ecclesiastes 3: 2) Only God determines that time.

Medically, after nine months of pregnancy comes birth. What triggers birth? Nobody knows. Doctors know that the baby, not the mother, makes the decision, but there are no clues as to how that decision is made, but the Bible has answered this question for us.

"He [God] determined the times set for them [all men coming into the world] and the exact places where they should live. (Acts 17: 26) The Bible asks this question of us - Is he (God) not your Father, your creator, who made you and formed you? (Deuteronomy 32: 6) I will answer this question for us,Yes, He is.

Through the guidance of the Holy Spirit we now go to the Bible to see examples of when God shut the womb.

Hannah - (I Samuel)

In I Samuel we read of Hannah who was married to Elkanah. The Bible says, "The Lord had closed her womb." (I Samuel 1: 6) Meanwhile her rival had children while Hannah waited, without even one. You may ask why did God shut her womb? God was waiting for the right time to bring that child from her womb to fulfil a specific purpose on earth.

When God shuts the womb, God is not saying, no you cannot have children; no, that is not His will, but he is saying that you should be patient for a while to enable Him to fulfil His purpose on earth. Hannah one day decided to draw the line. She went up to God in prayer. In her proper and beautiful passion for motherhood this desperate Hebrew mother cried unto her Lord in bitterness of soul. Hannah wept before God and prayed continuously to the Lord; she made a vow, saying, "O Lord, Almighty if you will only look upon your servant's misery and remember me and not forget your servant but give her a son, then I will give him to you Lord for all the days of his life. (I Samuel 1: 10-11)

This mother's prayer opened the door of her womb, because for the first time since she started praying, she prayed God's will for that child in her. God heard Hannah's prayers for the Bible records that "the Lord remembered her." So in the course of time Hannah conceived and gave birth to a son. (I Samuel 1: 19-20) This woman now by her promise gave God the opportunity he wanted to raise a leader for his people in a strange and difficult time.

Many women whose womb are closed may be women who want to bring children into the world to do their own will but God is saying, "that seed that I have put in you, I want it to be used for my glory. So mothers, what are your motives? I remember when I wanted a son. I prayed to God for a son and asked Him for a son who will be a man of prayer in His kingdom when he grows up. Within thirty day I was pregnant.

Therefore our motives matter a lot. Hannah received her child as soon as her prayers lined up with the will of God for that child.

So, mothers, I advise you to do this, if you have gone for many check-ups and tests and no reason is found as to why you are not conceiving, stop running up and down - maybe God has shut your womb. No man on earth can help you. The Bible says that what He (God) shuts no man can open and what he opens no man can shut. (Isaiah 22: 22)

Even the best specialists on earth will not be able to help you, until you line yourself up for God's purpose and will to be accomplished in your life. This is what I advise you to do. Sit down at home as a couple and have a chat over a cup of tea with God - I do all the time. You may ask where will you see God? The Bible clearly tells us that God is everywhere.

> "Where can I go from your spirit? Where can I flee from your presence? If I go up to the Heavens, you are there; if I make my bed in the depths you are there; if I rise on the wings of the dawn; if I settle on the far side of the sea; even there your hand will guide me, your right hand will hold me fast." (Psalms 139: 7-10)

I just went through this Bible passage to let you know that God is omnipresent - He is everywhere, He is with us all the time. He has promised never to leave us or forsake us. You may then again ask- how will you know that God is with you and is hearing you? God himself told us to come to him and we will reason together (Isaiah 1: 18).

Imagine the God of the universe reasoning with us. But it is all true - I have done that many times. You need faith or trust to believe and know that He is there with you and once you believe that, God will speak back to you in your spirit to let you know He is with you. You may feel silly talking like that, but that is okay, as you will get used to it.

The Bible says God's ear is not too dull to hear you Isaiah 59: 1, which means that God has an ear to hear, so speak to him. If He is the one that shut that womb, He will instruct you and tell you what to do. When He instructs you, you must obey Him, for in obeying Him there is a great reward.

Examples of women in the Bible whose wombs were also shut

> Rachel's womb was shut but after much prayer God opened it. (Genesis 30: 22-23)

133

King Abimelech

This king took Sarah, Abraham's wife. God was not too happy about this. The Bible records in Genesis 20: 18 that: "the Lord had closed up every womb in Abimelech's household because of Abraham's wife Sarah." Even Abimelech was infertile because God had to heal him too when He forgave him.

Curses

A curse is a form of punishment, divine or supernatural that invokes harm or misfortune to a person in response to it. A curse can come as a result of disobedience to the Word of God or as a result of sin or family sin which children may not even be aware of. God pronounced many curses and blessings in the Bible in obedience or disobedience to His commands - for example, Deuteronomy 28 contains a list of blessings and curses for obedience or disobedience. This is an example of a curse: "You shall not worship any other God except the Lord. Cursed is any man who cast any image or cast any idol - a thing detestable to the Lord." (Deuteronomy 27: 15) In disobedience to these command, a curse on the fruit of the womb. (Deuteronomy 28: 18) Blessings also are pronounced on the wombs of those who serve him. (Deuteronomy 28: 4) God's Word tells us that provided His people do not bow down before other gods or worship them or follow their practices (Exodus 23: 24) "there shall be none barren [among His people]." (See also Deuteronomy 7: 13)

Lack of fruit bearing is a curse (Deuteronomy 28: 18), things like wickedness, disobedience to parents, idol worship witchcraft, crystal ball gazers, Ouija boards, palm reading, freemasonry, etc., all bring down curses upon people. A lot of people are victims of family curses, visited on them without even knowing what their great-grandparents were involved in. Insurance companies know about those curses, that's why they ask for medical reports, etc., before giving insurance to people. They do not know these things are curses, but they surely know that certain family weaknesses are passed down from generation to generation. Infertility can run in a family as a curse.

Take a biblical example. Abraham's family problem started with Sarah. She was barren for almost ninety years; then her son Isaac married Rebekah and she was barren for twenty years (Genesis 25: 21); then Jacob married Rachel and she was also barren. (Genesis

29: 31) So we see all these men attracted to women who were barren, but Abraham was under the covenant of blessing, God had already blessed him and all these women later went on to have children, because of God's faithfulness to His Word. The curse can be destroyed from operating in one's life by taking the following steps:-

- ❖ Embrace Jesus Christ as your Lord and Saviour.
- ❖ Accept Jesus Christ and the blood he shed on the Cross for you.
- ❖ Repent and forsake any known and unknown personal or family weakness or sin.

Not serving God

A decision not to serve God or acknowledge who He is and to reject Jesus Christ can led to infertility by bringing a curse upon such persons.

God told His children that they should "worship the Lord your God and His blessing would be on your food and water and none would be barren in your land." (Exodus 23: 25-26) This shows that fruitfulness is tied up to serving God. The Bible says:

"You have forgotten God your Saviour, you have not remembered the rock your fortress, therefore though you set out the finest plants and imported vines, yet your harvest will be nothing." (Isaiah 17: 10-11)

This passage clearly addresses those who have rejected God, even the best doctors in the world will not be able to help any man who turns his back on God. No harvest is what God promises such people; until they come back to Jesus Christ and submit to His authority, they may never conceive. You may then again say there are millions of people not serving God yet they are blessed with children, why me? The Bible answers that question like this for us-"The sins of some men are obvious, reaching the place of judgement ahead of them; the sins of others trail behind them. (1st Timothy 5:24)

A life without prayer

A person who does not pray could find themselves held in bondage for a long time because prayer is the only thing that changes situations.

If you notice, in the Bible all the couples who faced infertility were able to overcome it through prayer - Abraham prayed (Genesis 15: 1-5), Isaac prayed (Genesis 25: 21), Rachel prayed (Genesis 30: 22), Hannah prayed (I Samuel 1: 10), Manoah prayed (Judges 13: 8), Elizabeth and Zachariah prayed (Luke 1: 13); and through prayer God turned their situation around and blessed them with children. In his book, *Prayer Power*, my pastor Matthew Ashimolow called prayer, "The Christian's pilgrim staff to walk with God always. It is a mine that is full of rich supernatural minerals to be brought out, a Heaven unroughed by storm. When we are engaged in prayer, we discover the fact that it is the root, the foundation and the mother of a thousand blessings." From this quotation we can clearly see that anyone who says that they are walking with God, and yet do not pray, are deceiving themselves. You cannot walk a fruitful walk with God without prayers. The foundation of your blessing is not laid so how can you give birth to a thousand blessings?

Today I encourage you to start praying if you have not been praying. In prayer you start to give birth to all your blessings. In prayer you are able to boycot the natural realm and get into the supernatural.

What is prayer?

Personally I have found prayer to be the chain that links me to God. I have found prayer to be like the umbilical cord, the rope-like structure connecting the foetus to the placenta that supplies oxygen and nutrients from the mother's own circulation. As long as that baby is the womb, the baby remains connected to the mother through this cord for oxygen and nourishment. I have also found that as long as I remain in Christ I must stay connected to God, through the cord of prayer. Through this connection I am well nourished and cared for, well protected from all harm and danger, well-equipped for every good work.

Personally, prayer is where I live; the very breath I take every day is prayer. I have discovered prayer to be something wonderful and alive. I have no rules attached to where I must pray. I pray all the time and everywhere. I manage what quiet time I can as a mother of two little children. It is not always easy to find quiet times. But I have not allowed this to stop me praying. I pray always, before I start, I always tell the Lord to pick the prayer from the children's noise. To His glory, all these prayers are always answered. My two year old loves to pray so he always comes when I have my quiet time. He thinks it is singing time - not praying time; so no rules, we just keeping praying and God keeps answering.

My advice to you

This advice is especially for mothers with little children or those who don't have time to pray at home. Always make an effort to pray, no matter where you are, and make time to spend quiet times with God, even if you commune with God for only five or ten minutes a day. Then pray while you do other things around the house or office, quietly or in your spirit. I believe if you desire to pray the Holy Spirit will help you with a plan of prayer suitable for you. But pray always; prayer changes everything.

A family of seven brothers all under a curse of infertility (Matthew 22: 25)

I asked the Holy Spirit to show me examples of male infertility in the Bible and this was one of them:

> Now there were seven brothers among us. The first married and died, and since he had no children, he left his wife to his brother. The same thing happened to the second and third brothers, right down to the seventh. (Matthew 22: 25-26)

The Lord told me that this family had a curse of infertility. All men in the family were infertile. Notice the wordings carefully: "He died...he had no children." The same thing happened to all seven of them. Why? Because none of them prayed to reverse the curse. Prayer changes everything. When you pray mountains come down, situations change Prayer and praise are the Christian weapon of warfare. There is nothing on earth that cannot be conquered by praise and prayer. This family of seven brothers could not pray and they all died without leaving any issue simply because they would not pray.

Another biblical example of male infertility is found in Genesis 20: 17: "Then Abraham prayed to God, and God healed Abimelech, his wife and his slave girls so they could have children again." God had rendered Abimelech infertile because of taking another man's wife.

Emotional factors

Emotions can be blamed for some causes of infertility. The Holy Spirit has actually shown me some of the emotional factors that are likely to hinder fertility in the lives of people. Medically it is believed that excess stress can lead to impotence and reduce sperm count in men although this is difficult to quantify. It is generally thought that emotional trauma can account for ten to fifteen per cent of cases of infertility.

Worry, anxiety

All these can lead to infertility by shutting down the body's system and causing it not to function properly. During my research for this book I discovered that all the couples who faced infertility were victims of one or all of the above symptoms. God did not design our body system for worry. The Bible tells us to: "Cast all our cares on the Lord because he cares for us." He told us: "Cast all your anxiety on him because he cares for you." (I Peter 5: 7) The Lord Jesus Christ asked us this question: "Which of you by worrying can add a single hair to his life?" I want to ask you a question - how will your worrying produce that child which you desire? Many couples reading this book can testify that their worrying about this problem has not in any way helped them. The Bible says that, "A calm and undisturbed mind and heart are the life and health of the body." (Proverbs 14: 30)

The Bible says: "A glad heart makes a cheerful countenance, but by sorrow of the heart the spirit is broken. (Proverbs 15: 13) Just from these two Bible passages you can see that worrying destroys the body system. A calm and undisturbed mind and heart are the life and health of the body. So when worry sets in it starts to destroy the life of the body; it releases toxins into the body. Worry breeds more worry until one is almost going out of one's mind because of it. The Bible says that it breaks the spirit. Once a man's spirit is broken he is finished - the body becomes weak, the mind starts to play games, the body system becomes clogged up, and many organs in the body are affected.

The Holy Spirit told me that worrying and anxiety lead to infertility because the body system is not relaxed and a baby needs a relaxed atmosphere to implant itself in the womb. Please stop worrying and cast all your cares upon the Lord. God really cares for you and will surely bless you if you stop worrying and trust Him for all your needs.

Bitterness and unforgiveness

Bitterness - Many people have become infertile today because of bitterness. Bitterness is equivalent to sin for Peter said in Acts 8: 23, "for I see you are full of bitterness and captive to sin." When bitterness comes, it takes along its neighbour, sin. A bitter person always thinks his or her bitterness is justified - "Oh you don't know what he or she did to me!" Such people do not realise that bitterness will cost them more than what those people did to them. The Bible warns us thus: "See to it that no one misses the grace of God and that no bitter root grows up to cause trouble and defile many. (Hebrews 12: 15) When a bitter root is growing many are defiled. Do you think bitterness is hindering you from conceiving? Are you bitter towards someone?

What is to be bitter? Bitter is distressing, caustic, galling, an expression of severe grief.

What is a root? It is the (underground) part of a flowering plant that usually anchors and supports it and absorbs and stores food; the end of a nerve near the brain and spinal cord.

I can say a bitter root is the equivalent of a severe, bitter, distressing enemy that absorbs all of the flowering part of your body.

You can see that if the root of bitterness is growing in a person it starts to spread all over the body. So how can bitterness and a baby grow together? You must choose what you want to grow in your body, either a baby or bitterness - one must give way to the other. When bitterness grows it devours many things; this includes the child that you are desiring. Do you think you have given a bitter root room to grow in you womb and replace your child? All the organs in the human body work together to maintain our lives but if bitterness is growing in our bodies the effective working of our body organs is affected. God is asking you to forgive that person, no matter what they may have done to you. If you find it hard to forgive, ask God to help you. If you are sincere He will help you. That may be all you need to do in order to conceive.

A malicious and unrepentant heart

The Bible records the sad case of Michal, King Saul's daughter and the wife of King David, who died barren. The Bible records in II Samuel 6 the tragic story of this woman. Her husband, King David went to bring back the Ark of God from the house of Obed-Edom to the city of David, and there was rejoicing and dancing before God.

King David, wearing a linen ephod, danced before the Lord with all His might, while he and the entire house of Israel brought up the Ark of God with shouts and sounds of trumpets. As the ark of the Lord was entering the City of David, [his wife] Michal, daughter of Saul watched from a window. And when she saw King David leaping and dancing before the Lord, she despised him in her heart. (II Samuel 6: 14-16)

When David returned home to bless his household, Michal [his wife], daughter of Saul came out to meet him and said, "How the King of Israel has distinguished himself today, disrobing in the sight of the handmaids of his servants as any vulgar fellow would.".…And Michal daughter of Saul had no children to the day of her death. (II Samuel 6: 20, 23)

Why? She despised God and despised her husband. She had no place for God in her heart. She despised a man for worshipping God. She hated her husband, she did not reverence or cherish him one bit. She did not have a repentant heart - not even once do we read of her asking God to forgive her or asking her husband to forgive her. We do not read once about her praying for God to bless her with children like Hannah did, or Rachel or Manoah etc. All of the other women of God who were childless, prayed and the Lord later blessed them with children.

Michal died barren because she hated her husband, she hated God, she was too proud to apologise and too proud to pray. In contrast we read and know that David was a man with a repentant heart. If he had offended Michal he would have repented and the Bible would have recorded it.

The Bible says God is faithful and just to forgive us for all unrighteousness, But we must pray and ask him to forgive us. If Michal had asked, God would have shown her mercy, but pride did not allow her to, therefore she died barren. So listen, women; if you are a woman who always despises your husband and other people around you, you have no place for God in your life. If you are doing all these things and have difficulty conceiving, maybe you have a lot of apologising and repenting to do. Ask your husband and those you might have hurt to forgive you and then ask God to wash and cleanse you with the blood of Jesus Christ. This may be all you need to do and before you know it you will be pregnant in Jesus' name.

Some people want to argue, "Well, I know women who beat their husbands and still have lots of children. Well, you better forget those people and settle your account with God; it could be that their sins have not caught up with them as yet, but they will later. If a woman with children beats her husband and insults him, later on in life, she will be shocked to find all those children doing the same to their spouses. She may well live to regret her ways. For you can start afresh and raise a family that will bring glory to God on earth.

When I first knew the Lord and gave my heart to him, I would see some of my friends doing certain things and I would say, "Oh, let me try doing this too," and the Lord would clearly warn me, saying: "Vero do not try it, for you will not get away with it." The voice of the Lord helped to restrain me because I knew I could not get away with doing the same things that others were doing. God deals with us individually, one person may do something and keep getting away with it, while another could try it and face dire consequences. So let us remain broken and repentant so that God's blessing may continue to flow in our life - let us not be like Michal.

The blessing of a repentant heart - Sarah

The Bible records in Genesis 11: 30 that Sarah, Abraham's wife was barren and bore him no children. Then God said to Abram: "I will make you into a great nation and will bless you. (Genesis 12: 2) After God had spoken and revealed His will to this couple, Sarah took no heed and she quickly devised her own plans. She told Abraham to sleep with her maid to enable her to build a family. Abraham agreed to this plan and went to be with Sarah's maid, Hagar, and she conceived. Abraham did not take a stand on the Word that God spoke to him.

When Hagar conceived that is when the real war began in Abraham's house. In Genesis 16 we read of fighting and quarrelling between Sarah, Hagar and Abraham himself. Talking about Sarah, we read of a woman who laughed when God told her He would bless her and make her a mother but later she was quick to admit that the joke was on her. (Genesis 18: 12, 15)

We read of a woman who agreed time and again to go with other men at the suggestion of her husband. (Genesis 12: 11-15, 20: 1-3) We read of a woman who did not think twice before giving another woman to her husband and we read of a husband who never gave a thought to the fact that his wife could be raped or sexually abused. We read of a couple, especially of a woman, who did not take the promise of God seriously. We read of a woman who loved fighting. We read in Genesis what Sarah finally did to Hagar after Isaac was born. One day the son of the slave woman mocked Isaac (his name was Ishmael), the offspring of a failure of faith. It was now necessary for Hagar and Ishmael to be sent away for they could not have a part in the purpose of God, which God had planned to achieve through His chosen people.

We read in the Bible how Sarah handled this issue, she said to Abraham: "Get rid of that slave woman and her son for that slave woman will never share in the inheritance with my son." (Genesis 21: 10) This was the same woman on whom Sarah had built her hopes of raising a family. She did not care any more. She was now a mother, she had Isaac. Can you imagine the scene that day in Abraham's house as Sarah made sure she got her way? The Bible records that this matter distressed Abraham because it concerned his son, Ishmael. (Genesis 20: 11) I am sure Abraham was ready to deal severely with Sarah that day; after all she was the one who persuaded him to sleep with Hagar. She was the one who created the terrible situation in the house, but thank God for His mercy. That day God intervened in that family to bring peace back to the home. God said to Abraham: "Do not be distressed about the boy and your maidservant. Listen to whatever Sarah tells you." (Genesis 21: 11-12) So Abraham listened to God, and did what Sarah said, and sent Hagar and Ishmael away.

Whilst all this was going on, God was working in the life of Sarah and Abraham. It took many years but the Bible says, "God changes us from glory to glory." At times it looks slow but God takes His time to accomplish His purpose in our lives. God could easily have given Sarah a child, when he gave Hagar Ishmael, but I have since learnt that God cannot be blackmailed or bullied into doing anything. God had to accomplish His perfect will in Sarah's life. The Bible records that Sarah obeyed Abraham and called him her master. She changed into a new woman, and she even obeyed her husband and submitted to him. Thus God blessed her and also said to us women that we will be Sarah's daughters, if we do what is right and do not give way to fear. (I Peter 3: 6) Sarah was blessed by God and she lived in peace and brought Isaac up in a godly home without quarrelling and fighting; God had finally finished His perfect work in her life. I want to advise husbands and wives, if they are still playing cat and mouse like Abraham and Sarah, that they might be the ones delaying their child from coming. God may just be waiting for them to put their houses in order and to create an atmosphere conducive for those special children he wants to give to them. He may not want such a child to be born into a household where the child will witness his parents fighting and wrestling with each other.

Isaac was a special child, God wanted him to be born into a peaceful and godly home. Your forthcoming baby may be the same, so get your home in order.

Many people will say, "Well I know a lot of couples who fight every day and yet they have children." Please, I advise you to forget those people; if they are fighting and have children, this is not your portion. Therefore do not concern yourself about them - for every man will reap what he sows. I cannot emphasise enough that both of you must make a commitment to God to help you to change and bring peace into your home, in Jesus' name, Amen.

Isaac - a blessed man

God's initial preparation for the coming of Isaac into Abraham's home paid off. Reading through the Bible, he is one of the few men who really loved his wife. The Bible records that Isaac brought her into the tent of his mother, Sarah, and married Rebekah. So she became his wife, and he loved her. (Genesis 24: 67)

After this marriage, Rebekah did not get pregnant for almost twenty years - what did Isaac do? Did he marry another woman, have concubines? The answer is no. The Bible records that Isaac prayed to the Lord on behalf of his wife because she was barren.

The Lord answered his prayer and his wife became pregnant. (Genesis 25: 20-21) What a man! Mothers, I pray that you will make your home a place of peace and love where you can raise up great husbands like Isaac, men who will pray for their wives in both difficult and good times.

Impatience

One of the causes of Infertility is impatience. While researching for this book, I discovered that a lot of couples were unwilling to try for any period of time before embarking on a fertility treatment. Their doctors may say to them, "Wait a little longer, try for some time first," but they, being unwilling to wait a little longer, embark and pay thousands of pounds for fertility treatments that end up not working. They fail to achieve a conception, lose a lot of money and come back home broken and battered, both physically and emotionally. The tampering with the body, especially a woman's body, in most cases ends up creating problems that were not in existence before the treatment was embarked upon.

One of the things I have learnt to cultivate whilst walking with the

Lord is patience. No human being can walk a fruitful walk with God, without patience. The Bible clearly tells us that there is a waiting time. "those that wait upon the Lord, shall renew their strength, they shall mount up with wings as Eagles, they shall run and not be weary. They shall walk and not faint." (Isaiah 40: 31)

While you wait on God, He will renew your strength, He will encourage you and strengthen you, He will give you an assurance that everything is under His control. Humble yourself, therefore under God's mighty hand that He may lift you up in due time. (I Peter 5: 6) There is a due time with God and when the time is due nothing will stop that child from being born in Jesus' name.

Wickedness

This is another cause of infertility among so many today. In Deuteronomy 27, there are many curses and all of them involve one form of wickedness or another. One example is this: "Cursed is the man who withholds justice from the alien, the fatherless or the widow." (Deuteronomy 27: 19) The Bible says in Proverbs 3: 33: "The Lord's curse is on the house of the wicked, but he blesses the home of the righteous. One of these curses is the curse of the fruit of the womb (Deuteronomy 28: 18). "The way of the wicked is like deep darkness; they do not know what makes them stumble. (Proverbs 4: 19)

From this passage of scripture we can see that the wicked man knows he is falling, but he does not know what makes him stumble and fall. The Bible says the house of the wicked will be destroyed, but the tent of the upright will flourish. (Proverbs 14: 11)

"House of the wicked" includes their seed, their children, their womb, eggs, sperm and everything that pertains to them, for the sacrifice of the wicked is detestable to the Lord. In Hosea 9, God spoke about the penalty of wickedness. "Because of their wickedness in Gilgai I hated them, Because of their sinful deeds. I will drive them out of my house. Their root is withered, they yield no fruit." (Hosea 9: 15-16, Proverbs 15: 8) From these Bible passages you can see there is no hope for a wicked man until he turns from his wicked ways back to God. We now go to the Bible to read about infertility due to wickedness.

This story is found in Genesis 38 about Judah, his sons and Tamar, their wife. It is a case of male infertility due to wickedness. Judah had two sons named Er and Onan. "One day Judah took a wife for his eldest son; her name was Tamar. Er, Judah's first-born, was wicked in the sight of God, so the Lord put him to death. Then Judah said to Onan his second son, 'Marry your brother's widow, live with her and raise offspring for your brother.' So whenever he lay with his brother's widow, he spilled his semen on the ground to keep him from producing offspring for his brother. What he did was wicked in the Lord's sight so he put him to death also." We see two brothers whose wickedness robbed them of their seed. They used their own wickedness on themselves. They died without having any children, for the Word of God says, "both were wicked men". No wonder the Bible says, "the house of the wicked will be destroyed." (Proverbs 14: 11)

Note here that Tamar was not infertile - she was a good woman who married evil men. She was sent away with a deceptive promise by her father-in-law, back to her own family for many years, and was forgotten by the family she married into.

One day she heard that her father-in-law was passing by her village on his way to shear his sheep. She disguised herself and went out and her father-in-law thought she was a prostitute and slept with her. That same day she became pregnant. The Bible says, "about three months later Judah was told, your daughter-in-law, Tamar, is guilty of prostitution and as a result is pregnant." Judah said: "Bring her out and burn her to death." Then she bought out the seal and cord which her wicked father-in-law had used to pay her for sex on that day, thinking she was a prostitute. She said, "I am pregnant by the man who owns these. See if you recognise them." Then Judah recognised them and said, "She is more righteous than I am." From this story we learn of Judah's sons who were wicked men; both died childless because of wickedness. Er died without children, Onan had seed in him but he wasted his semen rather than produce children with it. What a shame. The Bible says that, "those who plough evil and those who sow trouble reap it." (Job 4: 8)

Therefore married couples who are finding it difficult to conceive need to check themselves for any form of wickedness as this could be the reason for their not having children at this present moment. You must examine yourself and repent of your wickedness. You say, "Is there hope for me?" "Yes, God says, 'If you return to him, he will return to you.'" (Zachariah 1: 3) God says, "I will restore you to health and heal all your wounds." (Isaiah 30: 26) Turning away from wickedness brings you back to God's blessing.

God is merciful; once you repent he throws away all the wicked acts you have done and puts the righteousness of Christ upon you. You become a new person in Christ.

Not faithful in tithes

One other cause of infertility is not bringing your tithes into the house of God. What are tithes? A tithe is literally ten per cent of your income. In the Old Testament God asked His people: "Will a man rob God or defraud me? But you say, "In what way do we rob and defraud you?" The answer is that you have withheld your tithes and offerings. You are cursed with a curse for you are robbing me, "even this whole nation." "Bring all the tithes [the whole tenth of your gross income] into the store house, that there may be food in my house and test me in this," says the Lord of Host, "and see if I will not open the windows of Heaven for you and pour out such a blessing that you shall not have room enough to receive it. I will prevent pests (disease, *sic*) from devouring your crops; neither shall your vine drop its fruit before the time in the field (miscarriage,) says the Lord of host and all nations shall call you happy and blessed for yours shall be a delightful land," says the Lord Almighty. (Malachi 3: 8-12)

There is a level of blessing attached to faithfulness in tithing. The Heavens are open to those who give and God's protection is upon them and their family. For a person who brings in their tithe, the blessing written above is upon them, but for those people who refuse to bring their tithes into the house of God, the devourer is let loose upon their life. Miscarriages, still births and infertility are just some of the curses upon those who do not tithe. You may say well that this was in the Old Testament. No, not by any means; our Lord Jesus Christ in the New Testament mentioned tithes - in Matthew 25: 23, in Luke 18: 12. In Hebrews 7: 6 - tithing was mentioned, confirming that even in our current generation tithing must continue. When you bring your tithe into the church or to the work of God, it helps to keep the Gospel going, and towards the help of the less privileged. But when you hoard what is meant for the glory of God you cheat only yourself out of God's blessing.

My personal experience

Because of my faithfulness to tithing, God's protection has been upon my home and my children. Three times the courts have sent bailiffs to come and take my house, but they have not succeeded because God's protection is on my home. Sickness is far from my home and my children, because of God's protection. I have never lacked anything, even what I will bless others with. God has continued to be faithful to me.

When the teachers at my daughter's school tried to put a label on my daughter, saying that she needed a "special school" in order to learn to speak, God immediately turned their report into foolishness. Within the term I received a letter from the same teacher telling me my daughter was the best girl in the school. Why? - because of my faithfulness in giving tithes and offering. I have received so many other benefits because of my tithing which I will share with you in my other books. I will encourage you to start tithing faithfully from now on.

If you are not sure about tithing, talk to God about this and he himself will minister to you concerning the issue of tithing. He will direct you in His wisdom about what you should do. God Bless You.

Sexual immorality

The Bible clearly warns us to keep away from sexual immorality, impurity and lust, which bring down the wrath of God. (Colossians 3: 5-6) Having many different partners usually leads to the infliction of such venereal diseases as gonorrhoea and chlamydia. They lead to inflammation and, if not treated early, could give rise to blockages, leading to infertility.

A promiscuous lifestyle could later on in life result in damage to the womb, blockage of the Fallopian tubes or even result in the woman becoming sterile. In the Bible, such acts as sleeping with one's daughter, sister, etc., carried a curse upon it. (Deuteronomy 27: 22) In the world today, many people do all these things and get away with it, but for some, they may not be so lucky, so if you find yourself caught up in any of these things, you may need to repent and tell God you are sorry and He will forgive you. This may be all you need to do to conceive.

Biblical examples of sexual immorality - Genesis 20

Abraham and Abimelech

Infertility due to sexual immorality - in Genesis 20 we read of Abraham and Abimelech. Abraham had left the south country of Negeb and arrived in Gerar. Here he told his wife to lie and to say that she was his sister, so Sarah lied and King Abimelech sent for Sarah and took her. Here was a king with so many wives, yet sexual immorality had bound him. He could not resist a beautiful woman but the Bible records,

"God came to Abimelech in a dream by night and said, 'Behold you are dead because of the woman whom you have taken as your own, for she is another man's wife.'" (Genesis 20: 3) Abimelech tried to explain to God that he was innocent in this matter, but God said to him, "Yes, I know you did this with a clear conscience, and so I spared you from sinning against me. That is why I did not let you touch her. (Genesis 20: 6)

God commanded the king to return Sarah to Abraham. When the king returned her to Abraham, Abraham prayed to God and God healed Abimelech and his wife and his female slaves and they bore children, for the Lord had closed tightly the wombs of all Abimelech's household, because of Sarah, Abraham's wife. (Genesis 20: 17-18)

Many will say, "Well! Everyone is sleeping with everyone and getting away with it." That's fine but for some people it may not be that easy. If you are involved in sexual immorality, I will advise you to turn away from it and ask God to forgive you and heal you. God is faithful and just and will forgive you - in Jesus' name. Other biblical examples are:

If a man sleeps with his aunt, he has dishonoured his uncle. They will be held responsible. They will die childless.

If a man marries his brother's wife, it is an act of impurity; he has dishonoured his brother. They will be childless. (Found in Leviticus 20: 20-21)

King David (2 Samuel 11)

One of the greatest men who lived on earth did not escape the curse of sexual immorality. The Bible records that in the spring, at the time when kings go to war, David sent off his fighting men and stayed at home. One evening David got up from his bed and walked around on the roof. He saw a beautiful woman bathing and David sent for her. She came to him and he slept with her. Then she went back home. The woman conceived and sent word to David, saying, "I am pregnant."

This woman was Bathsheba. She was a married woman, and her husband was among the fighting men David sent off to war.

When David discovered this woman was pregnant, he sent for her husband to come back home from war so that he would go home and make love to his wife thus passing off the pregnancy to this man. When Uriah, Bathsheba's husband, came, David urged him to go home and wash his feet. Uriah said to David, "The ark and Israel and Judah are staying in the tents, and my master Joab and my Lord's men are camped in the open fields. How could I go to my house to eat and drink and lie with my wife? As surely as the Lord lives I will not do such a thing.

This man was a godly man. This man loved and revered God. He had respect for the king. His decision not to go home and sleep with his wife cost him his life, for when he went back to war the next day, King David sent him with a letter which carried his death sentence. He was put in the place where the battle was fiercest and was killed. David sent for his wife and married her.

God's judgement

The first thing that God told the king was, "out of your own household, I am going to bring calamity upon you. Before your eyes I will take your wives and give them to one who is close to you, and he will lie with your wives in broad daylight."

The second judgement was that the child conceived through that act of sexual immorality died. Then David comforted his wife Bathsheba and went to her and lay with her. She gave birth to a son and they named him Solomon. The Lord loved him. (II Samuel 12: 11, 24)

Solomon

Solomon was a son born to David through this marriage. He was blessed and loved by God, He ended up as the wisest man that ever lived. He was one of the richest men who ever lived and he had tasted just about everything life had to offer- He had beautiful women in his life, He was wise, lived a luxurious life style and had everything life had to offer at his disposal. He still ended up marrying seven hundred wives of royal birth and three hundred concubines. (I Kings 11: 3) So watch out for sexual immorality. If you escape infertility, your children could end up with sexual problems too much for them to handle and may not know it was your immoral behaviour that has been passed on to them.

At the end of all his sexual adventures I would like to leave you with a statement made by this great man. He said, "All is meaningless, meaningless, chasing after wind." (Ecclesiastes 1: 2) After sampling everything life had to offer this great man had only one advice to give to us - it proved meaningless. So, if you are wise, listen to the words of the most sexually immoral man that ever lived. It was not worth it.

Chapter Seventeen

More Questions On Infertility Answered From The Bible

What Of Infertility Among Christians?

During my research for this book I discovered that infertility affects as many Christians as non-Christians. I also discovered that most Christians had excuses as to why they were infertile, statements like, "God is using it to make us love him better", "serve him better", "teach us a lesson", "does not hear my prayer", were common statements made by God's people.

Today under the clear leadership of the Holy Spirit I have decided to answer some of the major questions asked on this issue. The first statement I am going to make is this: infertility among Christians can be attributed to one reason and that is *not knowing God's will and purpose!*

God himself said this in Hosea 4: 6 "my people are destroyed for lack of knowledge;" God did not attribute destruction of our lives and lack to the devil or infertility, he attributed it to lack of knowledge. When we lack knowledge of the will and purpose of God for our lives, then the consequences are great. From the day God created man on the face of the earth, His will and purpose was made clear: "Be fruitful and increase in number, fill the earth and subdue it." (Genesis 1: 28) When God took His people out of the land of Egypt, God again told them: "I love you and will bless you and increase your numbers. I will bless the fruit of your womb. You will be blessed more than any other people; none of your men or women will be childless." (Deuteronomy 7: 13-14)

In Deuteronomy 28: 4, God again confirms His blessing on His people: "the fruit of your womb will be blessed." Here we see God's desire and will for His people; the Christians - those who believe in Christ Jesus - God himself meets all their needs, supplies all their demands. Everything related to a Christian is to bear a mark of prosperity and success. God again speaks in Malachi 2: 5: "My covenant with him was a covenant of life and peace..." That is for every Christian, not only spiritual but physical life; His covenant with His people is one of life, not death - for a man or woman who believes in Him.

There is no way whatsoever that a Christian who believes these promises from God's Word can remain sick or infertile, because God's Word cannot fail. If God said, "...none of those who serve him will be barren," then that's exactly what it means: none means none to God. In Christ Jesus, God's promise to all Christians is fruitfulness - children - for the Bible says: "if a man remains in me and I in him, he will bear much fruit." (John 15: 5)

As long as you belong to Christ, God's promise to you is to have children.

My own personal experience of ignorance of God's word

In August 1992, I gave my heart to the Lord. Soon after this experience, burglars started coming into my home. Several times they came in and stole valuable things. Finally I cried out to the Lord to ask why this was happening to me. He then answered me by saying I was not releasing the ministry angels. Let's look at Hebrews 1: 14.

Are not all angels ministering spirits sent to serve those who will inherit salvation?

The ministrying angels are here to serve us but if you have someone sent to serve you what must you do? You must give them specific instructions as to what you want them to do. The Lord told me that it was ignorance of His Word that caused me to lose all those things through a thief. After that day I started instructing my ministering angels every day as to what I wanted them to do. Until the time of writing this it has been six years and no thief has ever come near my home. Glory be to God. His Word is true, it can never fail.

God created man to multiply and increase and subdue the earth. God gave man the power to have control over every situation in the earth. Man is to use the power of God's Word to change whatever situation he does not like.

Does God use infertility to make us love him more and serve him better?

This is probably one of the greatest deception of that enemy of man, Satan.

If he can get the Christians to believe this lie, soon we will have no more witness.

What will happen if Christians decide not to have children in order to serve God better? What would have happened if after God created Adam and Eve they decided not to obey God's command to multiply and fill the earth so that they can love *and serve God* better? The earth would have remained empty and you and I would never have been born. It is God's perfect will, His desire for every Christian to have children. Why?

To have a witness to the world

Christians must have children who will be witness to the world, bringing the gospel to the ends of the earth. If God denies the Christians children, soon no one would be left to carry God's message to the ends of the earth.

His blessings are tied up in our children

God himself is our Heavenly Father and also the Father of our Lord Jesus Christ; the Bible says that God so loved the world that he gave His only begotten son. Why? God knew the importance of children. When mankind sank into sin, God needed someone to help him restore mankind to him. God himself needed help and His son was there to help. No one knows more about the importance of children in our life than God himself.

For these are God's command to the children of Israel, His children.

> "These commands that I give you today are to be upon your hearts. Impress them on your children. Talk about them when you sit at home and when you walk along the road, when you lie down and when you get up." (Deuteronomy 6: 6-7)

We can clearly see that God's desire is to bless us with our own children, who we will teach His ways to and that they in turn teach their own children. God's blessing is meant to rest upon a thousand generations of those who love and fear him. (Deuteronomy 5: 10)

Abraham had a promise from God, that promise was a promise which involved the blessing of children.

152

"I will bless her [Sarah] and will surely give you a son by her. I will bless her so that she will be the mother of nations; kings of people will come from her." (Genesis 17: 16)

When King David who also walked with God wanted to build God a house, (temple) God said to him, "...your son whom I will put on the throne in your place will build the temple for my name." (I Kings 5: 5)

David was a man who loved God and served God, yet God blessed him with children. God had plans for David as well as His son. All God's plans are tied up with our children and loving and serving Him is also part of His plan. Having children does not stop us from serving God or loving Him. God himself said: "It is not good for man to be alone - I will make him a helper suitable for him. (Genesis 2: 18)

This God did by taking the ribs of the man and forming a woman for him. (Genesis 2: 21) Even this woman was not enough. God also commanded them to multiply and fill the earth. God loved Adam and Eve, he wanted them to serve Him, for the Bible records that "he came in the cool of the evening to the garden..." in order to be in fellowship with them. (Genesis 3: 8)

Having children does not in any way hinder one from serving God. Rather it enhances our service to God. The decision to serve God and not have children must be a personal decision for you, from your own heart (of your own will), because that is not God's will. If you feel not having children will make you serve God better, then that is what you should say, but please don't say it is God who is denying you children to enable you to serve Him better. That contradicts the Bible and the nature of God. Who said: "I'm the Lord, I change not."(Malachi 3: 6) The God who in Genesis said, "...everything produces after its kind and the seed is in itself." So God has already put the seed in you to bring forth children when you were born. There is no way that He will deny you that which He has promised you. Has the God who said, "None in my house shall be barren," changed His mind? *No* - He remains true and faithful to the end, No child of God will be denied his inheritance if he goes after it. For the Bible says: "Sons are a heritage from the Lord, children a reward from him. (Psalms 127: 3)

Question

"Before I became a Christian I had one (or more) abortions, which led to many medical complication in my reproductive

organs. Now that I am a Christian, will I be able to have children? What is my position spiritually on this issue?

Before we proceed with this question we must first find out the meaning of the word abortion. What is abortion? Abortion is the premature termination of a pregnancy by taking a foetus from its mother's womb. Abortion can be induced or may be spontaneous.

Medically induced abortion: this is where a woman consents to a doctor terminating the life of her unborn child. It may be medically advised, as in cases where doctors feel conditions exist that could endanger the life of the mother or child. Women who accidentally become pregnant and do not want to bring such a child into the world might also choose to have such babies aborted. Abortion is very common among the young women of our generation due to sexual promiscuity.

Spontaneous abortion

This is where a woman who is pregnant loses or miscarries the baby. Many reason are attributed to the cause of this.

The abortion I will be discussing here is induced abortion - where a woman deliberately decides to terminate the life of the child in her womb. The first statement I will make here is that, "Abortion is a heinous crime against God." Yes, each time a life is brutally taken away, it is a crime against God. For the Bible clearly says: " *Thou shall not kill.*" (Exodus 20: 13)

This question came up because I discovered that a lot of women in the church were worried because the abortion they had had before becoming Christians still haunted them. They also felt a sense of guilt about it. It is right to feel guilt about abortion because abortion itself is murder. Where a woman deliberately takes the life of her unborn offspring that is murder. It is a fact that criminal abortions usually performed by quack doctors in haste in ill-equipped offices are many times more dangerous to the mother than normal childbirth. It is the general testimony of legitimate physicians that even though the mother survives the shock of this terrible outrage against God and nature, she is often doomed to a life of suffering and misery - physically, mentally and morally. Hence the guilt experienced by so many of my sisters in the Lord, who have had one or more abortions.

Today I want to bring you the good news that, while abortion is wrong and a sin against God, by the blood of Jesus Christ, which He shed on the Cross, that abortion is dealt with. The power of the blood of Jesus removed all that separated you from God. That same blood that

Jesus shed for you has dealt with all your sins, and you are perfected by His blood. God does not remember your sins (abortions), not one of them, for the Bible declares what the Lord says: "...for I will forgive their wickedness and will remember their sins no more." (Jeremiah 31: 34) Every sin is forgiven because of the blood of Jesus. Every sin has been washed away and this gives you unlimited access to the very throne room of God.

the Bible says: "Now in Christ Jesus, you, who once were far away, have been brought near through the blood of Christ." (Ephesians 2: 13) The blood of Jesus has restored your relationship and fellowship with God. You stand before God as a righteous person; the Bible says that the blood that the sinless Son of God shed for you makes you perfect.

Today I want to encourage you, my beautiful sisters, to let go. At times it is more difficult for us to forgive ourselves even though God has already forgiven us. Forgive yourself and put that guilt under the blood of Jesus Christ and serve God with peace of mind. For who the Lord shall set free is free indeed. (I shall write a book on abortion in the future.)

Secondly now that you are a Christian you are now in the family of God, and the Bible declares all things are yours. In the Family of God, your Father is the Father who will never give His child a stone for bread. You have a Father who loves you with an everlasting love, a Father who gave His best in Jesus Christ to redeem you from sin and death. You are a blessed woman; in the family of God no one shall be childless. I want you to know today that If you will forgive yourself and ask God to heal or bless you with children, He will surely bless you. For the Bible says that He who ask receives. Remember God has forgiven you and He loves you. God bless you.

Question

What of those who refuse to have children beacause of childhood experiances?

There are those who make the decision not to have children as a result of childhood experiences such as incest, rape, multiple abortion, all these experiences might have planted fear in their heart. People who have had these dreadful experiences in their childhood often make inner vows, such as: "I will never have children in my life-time.

I will never bring children into the world to suffer what I suffered in my childhood." Many people become so afraid of a repetition of that which happened to them happening again to their children that they make decisions not to have them.

Today I bring you the good news that Jesus loves you and cares for you; He wants you to know that He is more than able to protect you and put right anything that is wrong in your life. Your decision not to have children through fears of the past is wrong. If you are a Christian and serving God, the blood of Jesus is able to heal you and restore you. The same blood is enough to protect any child or children you may bring into the world. The blood of Jesus is enough to destroy every curse that might have come as a result of the abuse you underwent as a child.

God has told us in His Word not to be afraid of anything. Time and time again he tells us: "Do not fear." Why? Because He has not given us the Spirit of fear. God wants us to be bold and strong and full of His love. He wants you to deal with all these childhood experiences that may still be a hindrance to your life. (2 Timothy 1: 7) He says He has not given you fear but love and a sound mind.

This is what I will advise you to do:

❖ Come to God by faith.
❖ Tell God all your hurts and fears.
❖ Ask Him to help you forget all those bad experience and to heal you and to forgive you, as well as all those who hurt you in the past.
❖ Ask Him to bless you with children; tell Him you believe He is able to protect your children from all the nasty experience you went through.
❖ Believe He has done it. Keep praising him for it. God Bless You.

Question

What does the Bible say about secondary infertility?

Secondary Infertility is where a woman has one child and then stops having children. Even though she may desire more, she finds herself unable to become pregnant.

Bible

In the bible we find so many promise of fruitfulness. The promises of God concerning having children is clear.

- And God said to them "be fruitful and increase in numbers"(Genesis 1:28)
- Your wife will be like a fruitful vine within your house; your sons will be like olive shoots round your table, thus is the man blessed who fears the Lord (Psalm 128:3-4).
- Sons are a heritage from the Lord, children a reward from him. (Psalm127: 3)

From this few scriptures we see that the greatest desire of God is for us to have children.

In the Bible we see a case of secondary infertility in the life of Leah. The Bible says "when Leah saw that she *had stop having children* she took her handmaid... and gave her to Jacob as a wife"(Genesis 30:9.) Leah gave her servant girl to her husband Jacob and she started having children through her. But the Bible records that later "God listened to Leah, and she become pregnant and bore Jacob a fifth son...Leah conceived again and bore Jacob yet a sixth son (Genesis 30:17-19). In this case of secondary infertility, we see that even though Leah had more than one child, she still faced a period in her life when she wanted a child and could not have any. As she kept on praying and crying out to God, He listened to the cry in her heart and her prayers were answered and God blessed her with more sons.

Today you may face secondary infertility. A diagnosis may have or may not have been made. Whatever the cause of secondary infertility I believe there is enough information in this book you are reading to help you conceive. Just go to the index section of this book and check what relates to you and use the principles written down there and apply it to your situation. It will work for you in the same way it will work for someone who has never had a child, or someone who has one or more and still desires even more.

Whatever your situation remember God loves you and He

wants you to be happy. For the bible says "He satisfies your desire with good things. (Psalm 103:5) God wants you to have good things. Children are good and it is Gods desire to bless you with strong and healthy children to the glory of his name. The Bible says, "No good thing will be withheld from those who love Him." Ask in faith and trust Him to be faithful to bless you with more children. If God did it for Leah, He is able to do it for you. Remember prayer changes every thing.

Question
What of infertility treatments among Christians?

Infertility simply means that a couple have been trying to conceive for a year or more without result. The issue of infertility treatment now comes up where a couple decides to seek help medically in an attempt to conceive. In doing this, a lot of test, medicines, surgical treatment and test tubes will be involved. A lot of money will also be involved and your strength and emotions will be taxed. Infertility is one area which the doctors will admit that they know very little of. Because of lack of light in this area, most of the time the cause of infertility cannot consequently be detected, and where it is detected medical attempts to solve it may fail. The reason for this is clear, as the Bible says: "the secret things belong to the Lord our God, but the things revealed belong to us and our children forever, that we may follow all the words of this law." (Deuteronomy 29: 29) The second thing is that the Word of God says in Ecclesiastes 11: 5 that, "As you know not the path of the wind, or how the body is formed in a mother's womb, so you cannot understand the work of God, the maker of all things." The area of fertility is a secret thing that belongs to God." That's why doctors cannot understand it all, there are still aspects of it that is secret and belong to God alone. Man has his part to play, and there has been a lot of medical advances in the last few years but there are areas no man should touch.

Infertility treatment is one of the most distressing, disruptive experiences you can ever go through. Recently I prayed for a lady who had undergone infertility treatment without success; she told me: "I went through so much pain I was afraid I was going to die." Anybody who has undergone these treatments will tell you it was no joking matter.

I personally believe God did not intend us to go through so much pain; that's why Christ bore all our pain on the Cross, I am sure it saddens God to see us go through this amount of pain over having children.

158

For the Christian couple, I guess the decision for them to undertake infertility treatment will be a hard one. There are so many treatments available today; the Christian couple will have to make a choice as to how far they are willing to go and what they are willing to try in order to conceive. Most of the treatments available are in total contradiction of the Word of God. How far you go and what you decide to do will be a choice you make here on earth and for which you may one day have to answer to God. The Bible clearly tell us God's will and promise to those who serve him. God told us in the Bible that, "none in his house will be barren." (Deuteronomy 7:14) God also promised that He would engender a difference between those who serve him and those who don't. (Exodus 33: 16-17) So, if the people in the world are doing all this stuff and the children of God are right behind them, where is the difference which our God promised us? Either God is lying or we are totally lost, but because we all know God can never lie it means we, His children, have lost ourselves somewhere. It is time for the children of God to wake up and take their place on earth which God has allotted to them.

Moses the servant of God knew a difference must exist between those who serve God and those who don't serve him. God told us in the Bible that, "none in his house will be barren." (Exodus 7: 14) God also promised that He will make a difference between those who serve him and those who don't. (Exodus 33: 17) If the people in the world are involved in all those treatments, the children of God who have accepted Jesus as Lord and Saviour, should be able to look up to God from where their help comes from. They should be able to advise the world that the answer is not in more embryo research, but in the Word of God. The Bible tells us not to be afraid of anything including infertility because our God will fight for us. (Deuteronomy 3: 22)

Our Lord Jesus Christ told us, "I have come into the world as a light, so that no-one who believes in me should stay in darkness." (John 12: 46)

For every child of God who knows Christ for themselves the promise is Light. God promises you Light so the darkness of infertility is not big enough to overcome you. Why then will you who have the Light start running up and down, instead of getting into the word of God and getting all the promises concering having children and praying untill you get a result? The Bible says, "Men cry out under a load of oppression, they plead for relief from the arm of the powerful. But no-one says, 'Where is God, my maker?'" (Job 35: 9-10) Most of the time when trouble comes

We run to powerful men like doctors, etc., to seek relief. We only come back to seek the face of God when all else has failed, when the arm of flesh has failed us.

You must make a decision to stay with the Lord who the Bible calls, "the Lord who heals you." The Bible commands us to do this: "Come out from among them and be separate." (2 Corinthians 6:17)

Let's take a Biblical example of a person who faced an illness and did not seek God first.

King Asa

The Bible says that Asa's heart was fully committed to the Lord all his life. Asa was a Christian. (2 Chronicles 15: 17)

> In the thirty-ninth year of his reign Asa was afflicted with a disease in his feet. Though his disease was severe, even in his illness *he did not seek help from the Lord but only from the physicians.* Then in the forty-first year of his reign Asa died and rested with his fathers. (2 Chronicles 16: 12-13)

One can clearly see that God was not pleased with Asa for seeking the help of man when God had promised "to be his healer" (Psalms 107: 20). Many Christian couples desiring or taking infertility treatment have not sought the face of God or spent enough time praying and studying the promises of God concerning having children, they have not meditated on the Word of God enough to get results, like King Asa instead of seeking the face of God first, they are now relying on the physician. God uses doctors to heal and bless His people. He uses them to heal and he also uses divine healing but His primary desire is that we come to Him first, that we acknowledge him first as our healer. We should be able to say: "Father, in whatever way my healing comes, I know it comes from you. You are the God who heals me. Whatever you direct me to do, that I will do. You are the one I look up to." The point I am making here is that in all sickness, we must first seek the face of God before going to anyone else - especially in the area of infertility where the doctors have limited light. When we hand everything over to God, He will direct you to a hospital or clinic, if he wants you to go to one, He Himself will be in the doctor or nurse who will be dealing with you. He will instruct them as to how best to help you. Yes God is able to do this

160

through the Holy Spirit. I would love to advise you that in whatever situation you find yourself try to acknowledge God first.

I am not putting down the work of doctors because they do great work. Millions of lives are saved by the dedication and work of doctors all over the world. The point I am making here is that no matter what happens our hope must be built on the Word of God and not on human beings. If we do that, God's blessing flows into our lives.

God's Word says to us: "Woe to those who go down to Egypt for help, who rely on horses, who trust in the multitude of their chariots and in the great strength of their horsemen, but do not look to the Holy one of Israel, or seek help from the Lord" (Isaiah 31: 1).

I want to leave you with these promises from the mouth of God - "You will be blessed more than any other people: none of your men or women will be childless" (Deuteronomy 7: 14).

Moses, the servant of God, asked God this question: "What else will distinguish me and my people from all the people on the face of the earth?" And the Lord said to Moses: "I will do the very thing you have asked, because I am pleased with you and I know you by name" (Exodus 33: 16-17). Moses, the servant of God, asked God to distinguish between those who didn't serve God and those who were God's people. God agreed with what Moses had asked and did just that.

The Bible says in Isaiah 31: 2: "He [God] does not take back his words." Has God changed? If you say no to this question, then you must also believe that His promise is sure and cannot fail. Below I answer two questions on the various treatments undertaken at the infertility clinics.

Question

What about *in vitro* fertilisation and embryo freezing?

In vitro fertilisation is a method of treating infertility in which an egg is surgically removed from the ovary and fertilised outside the body. *In vitro* means "in glass." This method of treatment is undertaken when the woman's Fallopian tubes are permanently blocked or absent, where the man's sperm count is low or where there are antibodies in the woman's cervical mucus which kill the sperm.

A woman undergoing this treatment will normally be given fertility drugs during the first eight days of her menstrual cycle; this is to stimulate her eggs to ripen. After some days the woman will go through a series of ultra sound scans to monitor the ripening of the eggs in her ovaries.

Immediately or before ovulation (which may be induced by drugs), ripe eggs are remove by laparoscopy or by ultra sound-guided-needle-aspiration through the vagina or abdomen. The eggs are mixed with the man's sperm in a dish which is then put in an incubator. Then the eggs are examined to see if they have been fertilised and have started to develop into embryos. Usually at the two or four cells stage, they are placed in the woman's uterus through the vagina. Recent research shows that half or more of all the eggs may have abnormal chromosomes and cannot develop into normal embryos after fertilisation. The eggs begins to divide but the pregnancy miscarries.

Freezing embryos (cryopreservation)

At the temperature of liquid nitrogen, -196° C, biological materials do not deteriorate. Once an embryo is placed in a glass tube and cooled to this temperature, it can theoretically be held almost indefinitely.

When used

Quite often more than three eggs are fertilised in a single IVF cycle but legally only three can be implanted at once. Many clinics now have the facilities for freezing the remaining embryo.

These methods are used:

A) When couples wish to keep them so that they can be used in the future.

B) Where embryos are produced but the mother reacts to the drug treatment in such a way that they cannot be immediately placed in her womb.

It is a fact that the process of freezing may in itself cause damage so that either the embryo may not grow properly or possibly the resulting child may experience some problems when he or she grows up to be an adult.

What the Bible says

The issue of IVF and embryo freezing is a very delicate one. A lot of people will argue and say, "Well, that was the only option left for me, to be able to have children." There are many things we do that are the only options left for us, and yet as children of God those things may be good, but they may not be God's perfect Will for us.

In the beginning of creation, God created every living thing and put it in its natural environment. God said:

"...let birds fly above the earth across the expanse of the sky." So God created the great creatures of the sea and every living according to their kinds, and every winged bird according to its kind...God blessed them and said, "Be fruitful and increase in number and fill the water in the seas, and let the birds increase on the earth." (Genesis 1: 20)

When God created the birds and fish, he put them in the natural environment designated for them. Now, when God came to create man let's look at the place where He put him. "And the Lord God formed the man from the dust of the ground and breathed into his nostrils the breath of life, and the man became a living being." (Genesis 2: 7)

Now the Lord had planted a garden in *Eden*. *What is Eden?* A place of pleasure, paradise, a place of glorious living, a place of delight or pleasure to the senses; a place where the temperature is right, the weather is good. The food is also delicious. Have you ever wondered why when it is hot people complain, and when it is cold people complain?

This is because when God first created man, he put him in a place where the temperature was perfect, a place of perfect living. Now we come to IVF and embryo freezing. A lot of people say the embryo does not have life yet. It doesn't feel pain so it is all right to freeze it. May I ask you a question? Are those embryos alive? Are they capable of becoming human beings? If you reply yes, it means they can feel pain as well.

I can boldly tell you that when you take a creature and place it in an environment contrary to its nature it is morally wrong. When you take a human embryo and freeze it for years, you are taking the laws of God into your own hands. The Bible says "the secret things belong to God. The things that are revealed belong to us and our children" (Deuteronomy 29: 29). Even doctors will tell you that they know very little in these issues that concern fertility. The doctors clearly admit that freezing embryos and IVF have their setbacks as the children born as a result could in later years be deformed or have disabilities that are incurable. The Bible says God himself determines the time every human being is to be born and the exact place in which they should live (Acts 17: 26).

When you freeze babies and want to bring them out at your own convenience, you are playing God. In freezing embryos you have now taken the place of God and you are creating life by yourselves. You have taken the secret things of God into your hands. I want you to know that, because something solves a problem or looks good, does not mean that we, as children of God, should dabble in it.

In every situation, we must let the Holy Spirit guide and lead us in the wisdom of God. God designed a perfect environment for a child in the womb of its mother; any other system that takes that child out of that environment and places it in any other environment is in direct opposition to the laws of God.

This is what I will advise my fellow Christian brothers and sisters to do. If you have dabbled in this worldly practice, repentance is in order. You must go on your knees and ask God to forgive you and also ask God to take such a child to become His own and heal every hidden disorder or abnormality that may exist.

God is faithful and just, and He is merciful, and He will forgive you and bless that child. *Do it today!* While there is still time. If you are not a Christian, God does not condemn you if you have done these things; He wants you to come to Him and He Himself will bless you and guide you. God loves you. He will forgive you and help you if you ask Him in faith.

QUESTION
What of donor insemination and egg donation for the Christian couple?

What is donor insemination?

This is where sperm from a donor rather than the husband is placed into the woman's vagina or womb, with the intention of fertilising one of her eggs. Love-making is not involved but tubes are the means used to transfer the sperms.

This method is used when:

❖ The man is not producing enough sperm or not producing at all.
❖ Where the man is carrying a genetic disease that could be passed on to his children.
❖ Where women who are not married wish to have children.

What is egg donation?

Egg donation is usually embarked on when the woman is unable to produce her own eggs. These could be as a result of:

❖ Her ovaries failing to work properly due to cancer treatment or some other problems.

- ❖ Where the woman have no ovaries at all.
- ❖ Where the man or woman cannot produce viable sperm or egg and a donated embryo is the only way for the woman to become pregnant.

To overcome these problems the woman now receives an egg from another woman, which could be used for fertilisation with her partner's sperms and the embryo placed in her womb.

What the Bible says

The first thing that we should get clear is that God created a man and woman to live together as one and multiply and have children in a happy environmental setting. A woman who does not want to marry should not be asking for sperm donation to enable her have children. Having children according to the way ordained by God is to be commenced after marriage. Where a husband and wife decide to employ the sperm or eggs of a stranger, who is not a party to their marriage, to father or be the mother to their children, this the Bible calls adultery. Why?

Is it adultery, even though physical intercourse is not involved? Where two strangers enter into an agreement to produce an illegitimate child, the act is illegal and immoral before God.

Reasons

The child born to such couples belong to another man or woman, not to the wife or husband.

No one knows what kind of blood is being introduced into the family.

The Bible says the sins of the fathers are visited upon the children to the fourth generation. Whose child is your wife going to be carrying? It could be the child of a mass murderer or even a Satanist or a person with a deadly disease and such weakness could be brought into your home. I know that God loves us and wants to bless everyone but the children of God must act in wisdom.

A lot of precautions are taken to prevent the receptor knowing who the donor is. Yet it is possible the unknown donor could trace the family and this could lead to blackmail.

The child may find out the circumstances of their birth and this could lead to low self-image, rejection or rebellion in later years. The husband or wife may, after that child is born, feel resentful towards the child because they know the child is not of their own seed.

Many Christians are asking questions on this issue and want to know what the Bible says. But from the scriptures it is quite clear that this is a reckless act of man. The Bible warns us of "taking the laws of God into our hands". "Has not the Lord God made them one? In flesh and spirit they are his. And why one? Because he was seeking godly offspring. So guard yourself in your spirit and do not break faith with the wife of your youth" (Malachi 2: 15). God made them one in flesh and spirit because he desires godly offspring from the two. Will you call the seed of a stranger godly offspring. Is that the plan of God for man?

Donor insemination or egg donation is committing adultery in the spirit. A life is created when the sperm from the male meets with the eggs of the woman. God made this possible in a healthy marriage environment. Where this event is done outside a marital relationship, making it possible for a woman to bear another man's child other than her husband, this is adultery; it also gives a single woman an opportunity to have a child without a husband and this contradicts the commands of God. He who gave the command, gave it to a man and woman, and not to a single lady. Why are we encouraging single ladies to have children on their own without marriage? This is wrong before our God. Adultery is a sin involving the body. The Bible warns us to, "flee from sexual immorality, all other sins a man commits are outside his body, but he who sins sexually sins against his own body" (1 Corinthians 6: 18).

Donor insemination or egg donation is a sexual sin, in the sense that the sperm or eggs of a stranger are being introduced into the vagina of another man's wife. Our Lord Jesus Christ said: "But I tell you that anyone who looks at a woman lustfully has already committed adultery with her in his heart" (Matthew 5: 28). So if only looking amounts to adultery what will you call the exchange of sperm and egg? This is not an issue to be looked on lightly, but it is an issue where you must honestly seek the face of the Holy Spirit and the Word of God. For a husband and wife to sit down and agree that the wife be impregnated by another woman's egg or another man's seed is a deliberate act of adultery because it is coming from their heart (from the spirit). For a single woman to sit down and decide to bring a child into the world by receiving the sperm of a stranger is a reckless act likely to incur divine displeasure. The Bible warns us thus - "marriage should be honoured by all, and the marriage bed kept pure, for God will judge the adulterer and all the sexually immoral" (Hebrews 13: 4).

Where you have gone wrong as a couple, repent and ask God to forgive you for your ignorance; God is merciful and forgives if we repent.

This is completely different from adoption where the couple have no part in the existence of that child. Let's look at adoption.

Question

What of adoption?

Adoption or to adopt is to take by choice into a new relationship, to bring up voluntarily a child of other parents as one's own child. Many people today have adopted children without home, orphans to give them a loving home and a new family. Adoption is good and right as long as a Christian couple does not consider it as an alternative to having their own children. One couple wrote that God wanted them to adopt; that's why he did not bless them with their own biological children. This statement is wrong in itself. While it is good to adopt, to assume that God has denied you children because he wants you to adopt is wrong. If God does this it means His Word to us, "That sons are a heritage from the Lord, children a reward from him" (Psalms 127: 3) is wrong. God cannot promise us something and deny us that thing. That is not the nature and character of God. Whatever he says, h e stands by it, and he does not change His mind. When you adopt a child and bring that child into your home, the protection and glory of God overshadows that child because you have taken that child as your own child. Be sensitive to the Holy Spirit to direct you, concerning the prayer needed for such a child, because there could be family weakness that child may have inherited from their biological parents which could surface later in life, if not dealt with properly in prayers. God himself says he is the father of the orphans. If God is the father of orphans, it in effect makes these little ones our responsibility to make sure they are well cared for and loved. I have just written briefly on this issue to let the Christian couple know that adoption is a godly and right thing to do; yet, at the same time, to let the Christian couple also know that even if they adopt, the will of God for them in Christ does not change. He still desires to bless them with their own biological children if that's what they desire. Esther, one of the great women of God ,who was used by God to deliver His people at a trying time was an adopted child. (Esther 2: 7)

Question

I am not a Christian - what are my chances with God on this issue?

Many of you reading this book may not be Christians and may be wondering if God can help you and hear your prayers because you are not a Christian. Well today I want you to know that God loves you and cares about you. If you make a decision today to accept Jesus Christ in your life as your Lord and Saviour, as soon as you say those prayers written in this book on how to accept Jesus, you instantly become a child of God.

God now gives you the same right as me and those who have served him for all their years. You are able to confess Jesus as Lord and take your place in God's plan for your life. The promises of God concerning having children and healing automatically become yours. Let us look at a woman who was not a Christian but made a decision to serve God and what God did in her life.

Setting up a blessing after infertility - Ruth

This story will challenge and encourage you and let you know that God is faithful to His Word and that the curse can be reversed and a blessing set up.

Under the leadership of the Holy Spirit we now take a journey through the pages of the Bible to the Book of Ruth to meet two great women and also to have a chat with Ruth, who rejected the curse of her people and set herself up for a blessing. Before we chat with Ruth I personally want to tell Naomi that she is a great woman of God. She lived a life worthy of emulation by all children of God. I can boldly write that without a Naomi there could never have been a Ruth. Naomi lived a godly life. She lived the life our Lord Jesus asked us to live; let your light shine before men, that they shall see it and give glory to our Father in Heaven.

Naomi was that light, her strength, quietness, and faithfulness to God produced faith in the heart of Ruth, which moved Ruth to accept God in her life.

Now we see Ruth; she was a Moabite woman, who married Naomi's son. After ten years of marriage her husband died. (Ruth 1: 4-5)

Naomi who was living in Moab, now decided to go back home to her people in Israel. She told Ruth to go back to her people since her husband was dead. Ruth found her heart closely tied to Naomi and she refused to be separated from her in the pathway that lay before her, choosing to share whatever the future might hold in store for the one on whom her love was set. The Moabites were cursed people, they were fleshy and carnal. We read in Numbers 22: 6, how the King of Moab sent for a prophet to come and curse God's people; the prophet could not curse them, but only bless them. When they could not entice this prophet to curse God's people, they then enticed God's people to fall into sexual sins. The Bible says, "while Israel was staying in Shittim, the men began to indulge in sexual immorality with Moabite women, who invited them to the sacrifice of their god, so Israel joined in worshipping the Baal of Poer and the anger of God burned against them." (Numbers 25: 1-3)

Ruth was coming from this type of background and when Naomi told her to go back to her people she now said these words to Naomi and set up a family blessing for herself and the whole world. "Where you go I will go; where you stay I will stay, your people will be my people and your God will be my God"(Ruth 1: 16). Alleluia! What a woman! The light of God had shone into her spirit. She rejected all that was not of God and chose to serve God and be with God's people. All I can say to this, is that this type of harvest in the kingdom of God can never be obtained by the witness of the lips; our lives must be vindicated and reinforced by the witness of our lives. Some daughters-in-law do not have a loving relationship and are always in a hurry to leave the company of their mothers-in-law because of their behaviour, but Naomi was different. What she preached she lived. May this example be our testimony in Jesus' name. Now we see the blessing that followed Ruth's statement: "So Boaz took Ruth and she became his wife; then he went to her and the Lord enabled her to conceive and give birth to a son"(Ruth 4: 13). The Holy Spirit told me Ruth was barren until she gave her heart to the Lord. She was under the curse of infertility for ten years of her marriage to Naomi's son. Note the words: - *"The Lord enabled her to conceive"* What does the word enable mean? It means to provide with the means or opportunity; to make possible, practical or easy. God made it easy for her. Ruth was infertile but God healed her, and made it possible for her to conceive. The day she said these words, *"your God shall be my God"*she set up an eternal blessing which the whole world including you and I are still enjoying. She gave birth to a son, Obed, who was the father of Jesse, who was the father of David, through whom Jesus Christ came into the world. God used that family to accomplish His plan and purpose on the earth and because of her wisdom she reversed the curse on her life. She had a whole book in the Bible named after her, so you see God is no respecter of persons. If you come to him He will bless you even more than you ever thought or imagined.God bless you and I love you.

Chapter Eighteen

The Fatherhood Of God

The dictionary describes father as a male parent of a child. He is also the first person of the Trinity, God; a man who relates to another in a way suggesting the relationship of father and child, to beget, to give rise to, to initiate, to accept responsibility for.

In this chapter, I would like to discuss with you the fatherhood of God. Many of us may have never thought of God as our Father, but God is the one who created us in His image. In the book of Genesis it reads: "So God created man in His image. In the image of God He created him; male and female, He created them. (Genesis 1: 27) You and I are made in the image of God. God is our Heavenly father, when you look at yourself, what you see is the image of God. You are created in *His* image. Today I want to let you know that God loves you and wants you to know that he is your Father. Our Lord Jesus Christ himself, in speaking about the Fatherhood of God, shared one of the most powerful Bible accounts with us to let us understand the Fatherhood of God.

Through the leadership of the Holy Spirit, I will like us to look into the Bible to read about the Fatherhood of God and even as you read I pray that the Holy Spirit quicken your understanding to comprehend and understand the Father who loves you and is calling out for you to come home.

There was a man who had two sons. The younger one said to his father, "Father, give me my share of the estate." So he divided his property between them. Not long after that, the younger son got together all he had, set off for a distant country and there squandered his wealth on wild living. After he had spent everything, there was a severe famine in that

170

whole country and he began to be in need, so he went and hired himself out to a citizen of that country, who sent him to his field to feed pigs. He longed to fill his stomach with the pods the pigs were eating, but no-one gave him anything.

When he came to his senses, he said, "How many of my father's hired men have food to spare, and here I am starving to death! I will set out and go back to my father and say to him: Father I have sinned against heaven and against you, I am no longer worthy to be called you son; make me like one of your hired men." So he got up and went to his father. But while he was still a long way off, his father saw him and was filled with compassion for him; he ran to his son, threw his arms around him and kissed him. The son said to him, "Father, I have sinned against heaven and against you. I am no longer worthy to be called your son." But the father said to his servants, "Quick! Bring the best robe and put it on him. Put a ring on his finger and sandals on his feet. Bring the fattened calf and kill it. Let's have a feast and celebrate. For this son of mine who was dead is alive again; he was lost and is found." So they began to celebrate. (Luke 15: 11-24)

Throughout the ministry of our Lord Jesus Christ, he was found among the needy, the sinners, prostitutes and those less privileged. The Pharisees and scribes murmured, saying, "This man received sinners and eats with them." He had already made a bad name for himself because of this. These Pharisees could not understand why Jesus received and talked with prostitutes and outcasts of any kind. It was a constant surprise to them that these people also loved Jesus. Those outcasts and needy people loved the Lord. In this parable of the lost son, Jesus explained why he loved these people. He told of the pain and love in the fatherhood of God. He told them of the father who had two sons and had lost one and because one was lost, he was more concerned about the lost son than the one who was safe at home. The point here is that something was temporarily lost, something of great value to the owner, and because it was lost, he was greatly concerned just as we would be if we lost a son.

For many of you reading this book, if you do not know Jesus Christ as your Lord and Saviour or God as your Father, I want to tell you plainly today, that you are the missing son or daughter that God is looking for. He is calling you to come back home to Him. He is the father who is sore for that lost child in a far away country. You may not care or have thought much about God and how He feels but I have now learnt that it is the one who loses the loved one that suffers most. It is the father or mother who suffers when their boy or girl has gone off into the world to pleasure him or herself. Oh, the pain and agony of a father or mother who would suffer any pain in this life, go to any length if it were possible, if by any means he or she could save that thankless child and bring him or her home! I want to relate this to you men and women who desire to have children today. What will you do if twenty years from now this same child you suffered to give birth to then turns his back on you and says: "No way, daddy/mummy; I don't love you any more." How will you feel? What will you do? Think about it. Will you give up on that son or daughter? Even if you will, God has not given up on you. The Bible says:

> "Can a mother forget the baby at her breast and have no compassion on the child she has borne? Though she may forget, I will not forget you! See, I have engraved you on the palms of my hands; your walls are ever before me." (Isaiah 49: 15-16)

He still wants you back, he is diligently searching for you until he finds you; he does not console himself for your loss by fellowship with people who have never sinned, he does not content himself by using others to fill in the blank. He is not a great employer of labour who can have fresh hands to take the place of the failures. No, says our Saviour Jesus, he is the Father, he wants you, he misses you. He goes after that which is lost until he finds it. The prodigal son came to his senses and decided to go back home to his father; he knew in his father's house he would have food to eat and shelter over his head. Today I also want to ask those of you who do not know him yet, will you come to your senses? Will you go back to the Father whose arms are empty, who aches for you, whose eyes are full of tears because of his love for you? Will you come home today?

Coming home

The prodigal son thought that when he went back home his father would treat him like one of his hired men, but how wrong he was. As soon as the father saw him coming, the father ran to him and said to his servants, "Quick, bring the best robe and put it on him, put a ring on his finger and sandals on him. Bring the fattened calf and kill it. Let's have a feast and celebrate, for this son of mine was dead but is now alive again; he was lost but now is found." So they began to celebrate. (Luke 15: 22-24) I have spoken to many people on the road as I go along, telling them about Jesus Christ and the love of God and they comment with statements like: "Oh, there are too many people in the world, why would God care about me? But I want you to know He cares. His arms are waiting for you to come home to Him. When the prodigal son came home he found all he was looking for at home; there was food to keep him warm, sandals for his feet, clothes on his back and a welcome party, and love too. When you come home, you will be coming back to the family of God, the God who said, *"In my house there shall be none barren."* (Deuteronomy 7: 14); the God who said, "there shall be no sickness in my house for I am the Lord who sent my word and it heals you." (Psalms 107: 20); the God who said, "I will create the fruit of your lips." (Isaiah 57: 19) That is the house you are coming back to.

All these words are most comforting to the children, if they believe them. But what of the Father - he wants *you* back. I have written powerful books on infertility and creative miracles - these books are written by the Holy Spirit himself to bring you healing and restoration and blessing beyond measure.

But going beyond all these blessings, listen to the revelation of the Father's heart not told by me or any man not even by the apostles, but by the only begotten of God, Jesus Christ who is in the bosom of the Father. He has revealed that it is God's loss more than yours when you go astray, that God suffers more than you suffer by your godless life, that he cares more than you care for your return to good. This may shock you but it is the truth; it may sound incredible to you and yet it ought not to be if we look, as our Lord Jesus bids us do, at the reflection of God in all human love.of God in all human love.

Today I advise you to come back home - the Father's arms are open, waiting for you. Come back home. You may say, how do I come back home? Read on to the next chapter - and find out how.

Chapter Nineteen

Who Is Jesus Christ?

The love of God led him to give Jesus Christ for the sake of you and me. His searching for us made him send Jesus to die on the Cross for us. The Bible says that, "God so loved the world that He gave His only begotten son, that whoever believes in Him shall not perish but have eternal life. For God did not send His son into the world to condemn it but to save the word through Him" (John 3: 16-17). Jesus came into the world to redeem us from the power of sin and death.

The will to choose abused

God created Adam from the dust of the ground and he became a living being. Now God planted a garden in the east, in Eden and there he put the man he had formed and the Lord God made all kinds of trees grow out of the ground - trees that were pleasing to the eye and good for food. In the middle of the garden were the tree of life and the tree of the knowledge of good and evil. The Lord God took the man and put him in the garden of Eden to work it and take care of it. And the Lord commanded the man, "You are free to eat from any tree in the garden, but you must not eat from the tree of the knowledge of good and evil, for when you eat of it you will surely die" (Genesis 2: 7-9, 15-17).

God created Adam with a unique ability to choose. He gave him free will and told Adam specifically, "You are free to eat from any tree in the garden but you must not eat from the tree of knowledge of good and evil, for the day you eat of it you will surely die" (Genesis 2: 17).

What kind of death was God talking about?

This was not physical death but spiritual death. Yet Adam did not obey God, for the Bible records that, "Adam and his wife ate of these fruit that God had commanded them not to eat. When the woman saw that the fruit of the tree was good for food and pleasing to the eye and also desirable for gaining wisdom, she took some and ate of it. She also give some to her husband, who was with her and he ate of it" (Genesis 3: 6). That disobedience brought death to the whole of mankind - why? - because we all were in Adam when he disobeyed God's instruction. You say: "How can that be possible?" Medically, it is a fact that a man produces ten million sperm cells a day in his testicles and each of these sperm is genetically unique. So in just six months only one man produces enough sperm to populate the whole world.

There is no doubt from the Bible account, that it is, "from one man that God made every nation of men, that they should inhabit the whole earth and He determined the times set for them and the exact place where they should live." (Acts 17: 26) There are a lot of theories about the origin of man but the Bible does not speculate on this issue. It is clear and simply written down for those who desire to know the truth.

After Adam's fall, we all fell with him because we all were in him. There was no other way for mankind to be saved again because the law requires that everything be cleansed with blood because without the shedding of blood, there is no forgiveness (Hebrews 9: 22). Jesus came into the world, led a sinless life in the world, and he shed His sinless blood on the Cross as an offering to redeem us from the sin committed by Adam. The Bible says

> Therefore, just as sin entered the world through one man, and death through sin, and in this way death came to all men, because all sinned - for before the law was given, sin was in the world. But sin is not taken into account when there is no law. Nevertheless death reigned from the time of Adam to the time of Moses, even over those who did not sin by breaking a command, as did Adam, who was a pattern of the one to come. But the gift is not like the trespass, for if many died by the trespass of the one man, how much more did God's grace and the gift that came by the one man, Jesus Christ, overflow to the many! (Romans 5: 12-16)

Adam brought sin into the world, Jesus brought the Grace of God into the world. Jesus came into the world, died on the Cross, shed His sinless blood on the Cross to redeem you and me from the sin committed by Adam. In His death he paid the price for the sin of all mankind; the curtain of sin that separated us from God was removed forever; Christ took our place and paid the price for you and me. Jesus Christ was sent by God. Mankind had fallen into sin and rebellion. Mankind had turned his back on God. "We all like sheep, have gone astray. Each of us has turned to his own way" (Isaiah 53: 6). No man sought God any more, sin had separated us from God. God had to do something to restore the fellowship between him and man. This made him send Jesus to come down to the earth and die on the Cross to redeem us from sin and death. Before we look at what Jesus did for us, let's look at the old covenant.

Old covenant priest

In the old covenant the high priest was the mediator before God and the people. He was the one who offered the animal sacrifice day after day first for his own sins and then for the sins of the people. He carried the blood of animals into the most Holy Place as a sin offering and the bodies of the animals were burnt outside the camp. This he did day in day out, yet the blood of goats and bulls could not take away sins, they remained an annual reminder of sin.

The high priest of Jesus Christ

When Jesus came as a high priest of good things that are already here, he went through the greater and more perfect tabernacle that is not man-made, that is to say, not created by man. He did not enter by means of the blood of goats and calves; but he entered the most Holy place once and for all by His own blood, having obtained eternal redemption. The blood of goats and bulls and the ashes of a heifer sprinkled on those who were ceremonially unclean sanctified them so that they were outwardly clean.

> How much more, then will the blood of Christ, who through the eternal Spirit, offered himself unblemished to God, cleanse our consciences from acts that lead to death, so that we may serve the Living God? (Hebrews 9: 11-14)

When Jesus came into the world, he saw that the sacrifice of animals for sin offering could not save mankind, so he decided to offer His own sinless body on the Cross and shed His blood to cleanse us forever from sin. This he did by dying on the Cross for us. Before Jesus could die on the Cross he had to live for thirty-three years on earth, and yet He was still without sin. The life of our Lord Jesus in its final perfection was a perpetual message to men concerning their unfitness to enter the divine presence. He lived a life of unbroken fellowship with God, which

176

we know we cannot do. His fellowship resulted from His being well pleasing to God (Luke 3: 22). His life on earth was acceptable to God, He did not fail or disappoint God so he was qualified to become the Saviour of all mankind. Nothing has ever separated man and God except sin. Jesus was sinless and so was pleasing to the Father and His death on the Cross dealt with our sin and made it possible for us to return to God. Our access to God at all times and under all circumstances is now open.

Draw near to Christ

Christ can only complete His work of saving men when they draw near to God through him. For Christ to do this there are two things which has priesthood is based upon. First we must make ourselves available to His priesthood and secondly submit ourselves to His authority. And in doing this we will find complete salvation for all things in him. It is only when men draw near that the priesthood of Jesus is operative in all their continuous activities.

Intercession

One of His duties as the Bible records is intercession, continuous praying without ceasing, because Christ is praying for us, our drawing near to him keeps us within His prayer cover, and through this intercession, we are being perfected and strengthened from day to day.

As this nearness is maintained, Christ our great high priest is the mediator through whom all the resources of the divine wisdom, strength and grace of God are communicated to us. We are being strengthened in our inner selves, growing up into Him; in all things our salvation to the uttermost is complete, to depart from nearness to God separates us from the protection of our high priest. This is a truth we must never forget. Standing alone, we are liable to be discouraged. But that brings us to the second truth, and that is that our nearness to God is through Him. It is through Him we draw near, and it is through Him that we abide in nearness. Thus the two places of His priesthood are in view.

The first is atoning, by which we draw near and abide in nearness. The second is intercessory and perfecting, that operates as we are near to God through His atoning work from day to day.

Let us draw near

"Let us draw near." (Hebrews 10: 22) Today I want to encourage you to draw near to Jesus Christ. Why? - because he has created the access which we need to get into the presence of God. This possibility of approach and access is the supreme fact resulting from the work of our great high priest. The one thing we are called to do is to draw near. There is no reason why we should not do so.

Every sin dealt with

Everything which excluded men from God was put away by Christ at His death on the Cross. The Bible records that on the day Christ was crucified, the sun stopped shining and the curtain of the temple was torn in two. (Luke 23: 45) Why was this curtain torn into two? This curtain was a symbol of that which had excluded man from God, through sin. In its rent condition it was the symbol of the open way to God.

Come the way you are

Therefore the appeal to us is not a call to prepare ourselves, or to make a way for ourselves to God, it simply says come, draw near, enter in. Our Lord Jesus Christ in John 6: 35 declared:

> "I am the bread of life. He who comes to me will never go hungry, and he who believes in me will never be thirsty. All that the Father gives me will come to me and whoever comes to me I will never drive away. For I have come down from Heaven not to do my will but to do the will of Him who sent me. And this is the will of Him who sent me, that I shall lose none of all that He has given me, but raise them up at the last day. For my Father's will is that everyone who looks to the son and believes shall have eternal life, and I will raise him up at the last day." (John 6: 35-40)

God's will was why Jesus came to the earth to give both physical and spiritual life to those who believe. He also promises that he will never reject anyone who comes to him. Many people think they need to stop sinning, go take a holy bath or do something before they can come to Jesus. Today I want to tell you, you don't need to do anything to come to him. Nothing is good enough except for you to accept His love and grace which he freely offers to those who believe in him. Most of the blessings written down in these books belong to those who belong to

Christ because, you see, it is He who paid the price to redeem us from the curses of the law which were hanging over us. On His death and resurrection on the third day, Jesus destroyed for ever all the curse and sin that hung all humans. But to avail yourself to this finished work you must come to Him and accept what He has done for you.

Don't wait until tomorrow

A lot of us put away doing the things we ought to do now thinking that tomorrow will be a better day to do them. You may say, "Oh, tomorrow I will give my heart to Jesus. Oh, tomorrow I will think about it." The great excuse for putting off till tomorrow what should be done today is that we hope that tomorrow we shall feel more like doing whatever it is. But we can never be sure of tomorrow, for it does not belong to any of us. Tomorrow belongs to God. Our Lord Jesus Christ illustrated this so well in the Bible account of the:

Rich fool (Luke 12: 16-21)

> "The ground of a certain rich man produced a good crop. He thought to himself, 'What shall I do?' I have no place to store my crops.' Then he said, 'This is what I'll do. I will tear down my barns and build bigger ones, and there I will store all my grain and my goods. And I will say to myself, 'You have plenty of good things laid up for many years. Take life easy; eat, drink and be merry.'" "But God said to him, 'You fool! This very night your life will be demanded from you. Then who will get what you have prepared for yourself? This is how it will be with anyone who stores up things for himself but is not rich towards God." (Luke 12: 13-21)

Look at this parable very carefully; many people in the world think that money can save them, but from experience we all know that this is untrue. We have seen the rich die without any of their wealth being able to help them. If you were to talk to them, I am sure they will tell you that they are still looking for peace and love in their lives. Yet the Bible says it is only in Christ that you will have real joy and peace on this earth. Now is also the right time; tomorrow may be too late. The day I heard that John Smith, leader of the Labour party was dead, I was so shocked. Here was a man who was preparing for the election, full of life on the television a few days earlier and the next we hear is that he is dead. This really brought it home to me; no matter what our plans are, they must be for *now*, for even the next hour does not belong to any of us.

Life is full of choices - every day when we wake up, we face choices; each choice we make carries a consequence and you alone have to live with your choice. The Bible says in Hebrews 3: 7-8 what the Holy Spirit says; "Today, if you hear His voice, do not harden your hearts, as you did in the rebellion during the time of testing." Please do not harden your hearts, choose Christ today. The Bible says *now*. God says, "Come now and let us reason together" (Isaiah 1: 18). For now is the accepted time, now is the day of salvation. The Bible tells us not to boast of tomorrow for we do not know what tomorrow will bring forth.

A wise decision

In this book I wrote of the ovulatory problems that women can experience, I used the Bible account of the noble man from John 4: 46-54. In this account we read of a noble man whose son was sick with a deadly fever. No amount of money was enough to save him; from the human stand-point all efforts had failed. This father heard of Jesus and came to him and pleaded with him to come and heal his son. Jesus did not go to his house as the man requested but gave him his word, saying, "You may go; your son will live" (John 4: 50). This father took Jesus' word and left and when he was going home, while he was still far off, one of his servants met him and told him his son was living and well. The father asked the time when his son recovered. He was told: "The fever left him yesterday at the seventh hour." The father realised that this was the exact time which Jesus had said to him, "your son will live," so he and all of his household believed. Here we see a wise father, a father who saw the might of the power of God's Word. This father had experienced the salvation of God, through what Jesus did, only by speaking His Word. This father belived and brought salvation into his own home. All his family believed. How many of you fathers today are willing to bring salvation into your home? How wonderful it is when the head of the house accepts Christ as Lord and Saviour for everyone in the house always follows the same trend. They all see the changes and want to do what daddy did. For many of you today I encourage you to be like the noble man; bring Christ into your home to be the Lord of your home and your whole family will be restored to fellowship with the Living God.

Today, I speak to you, my readers; if you have never known Jesus Christ for yourself, learn from the noble man, he became a believer in the Lord when the Lord saved his son from death. All his household also believed and received Christ. In this Bible accounts we see a family who faced impossible situations, and needed help which no human being could provide for them, which no money could buy. Christ did it for them and they believed. I would encourage you to believe in his love and his abilities to help you today. Christ gave them help and they believed. I will encourage you to accept Christ in your life today like the noble man's famliy did. The rewards are eternal.

Salvation

To accept him as your Lord and Saviour the Bible says that the Word is near you: It is in your mouth and in your heart; that is the word of faith we are proclaiming that if you confess with your mouth "Jesus is Lord", and believe in your heart that God raised him from the dead you will be saved. For it is with your heart that you believe and are justified, and it is with your mouth that you confess and are saved.

When you confess Jesus as Lord and Saviour you can pray in your own way, any way you know how, the simpler the better; the most important thing is your heart's condition.

Confession

Father, I repent of my sins and by your power I will no longer be a servant of sin. Father, make me your child. I believe that Jesus died on the Cross and that he shed His blood for me and that he rose from the dead on the third day. I confess and accept the Lord Jesus as my Lord and Saviour Lord; come into my life. Give me new hope and power to live for you. Wash me with your blood and sanctify me with your word and fill me with your Holy Spirit, to your praise and glory. Father, I thank you for making me your child. In the name of Jesus Christ of Nazareth, Amen!

Right standing with God

Immediately after the confession you now have right standing with God. The Bible says once we are justified through faith, we have peace with God through our Lord Jesus Christ, through whom we have gained access by faith into this grace in which we now stand. And we rejoice in the hope of the glory of God.

The Bible says, "as many as receive him, to them he gave the power to become the sons of God, even to them that believe in His name (John 1: 12). Once you have accepted Jesus Christ you now have a right standing with God and you are now born of the Spirit. This is the new birth.

He gives you the same benefits as those saved many years ago

Once you have accepted Jesus Christ as your Lord and Saviour all the benefits of the kingdom of God become available to you at the same moment; nowhere else can you receive such privileges. If a company employs you today, there is no way they will pay you the same amount or give you the same benefit as those who have worked forty or fifty years with them. But glory to God Almighty, He is no respecter of persons, the blood of Jesus qualifies you immediately for all of God's benefit.

Matthew 20

Our Lord Jesus Christ himself explained this himself in Matthew 20.

> For the kingdom of Heaven is like a landowner who went out early in the morning to hire men to work in His vineyard. He agreed to pay them a denarius for the day and sent them into His vineyard. About the third hour he went out and saw others standing in the market place doing nothing. He told them "You also go and work in my vineyard, and I will pay you whatever is right." So they went. He went again at about the sixth hour and the ninth hour and did the same.
>
> About the eleventh hour he went out and found still others standing around. He asked them, "Why have you been standing here all day doing nothing? "Because no one has hired us," they answered. He said to them, "You also go and work in my vineyard." When the evening came, the owner of the vineyard said to his foreman, "Call the workers and pay them their wages, beginning with the last ones hired -

and going to the first. The workers who were hired about the eleventh hour came and each received a denarius. So when those who were hired first came, they expected to receive more but each one of them also received a denarius. When they received it, they began to grumble against the land owner. "Those men who were hired last worked only one hour," they said, "and you have made them equal to us who have borne the burden of the work and the heat of the day." But he answered one of them "Friends I am not being unfair to you. Didn't you agree to work for a denarius? Take your pay and go. I want to give the man who was hired last the same as I gave you. Don't I have the right to do what I want with my own money? Or are you envious because I am generous? So the last will be the first, and the first will be the last." (Matthew 20: 1-16)

Reading through this Bible account spoken by our Lord Jesus Christ himself, I want to encourage you to come to God, for you have right standing with him now; what he will give to those who have walked with Him a hundred years He also gives to you. Many people may not like this; as you see, the labourers who came first were not happy when the land owner paid all the workers the same amount. They wanted more; a lot of people may tell you, "Oh, you are a new Christian, you must do this and that." I will advise you to come to God yourself. He will fill you with His Holy Spirit who will direct you and guide you in all your ways. He will help you when you need help. He himself will direct you to a good church where you will grow in His Word and have a family in the body of Christ. He himself will place the right people in your life, who will not try to intimidate you but will help you to walk in the way of the truth to seek God for yourself.

A new baby

God's desire is for you to grow up in His grace and come closer to him. Take an example; when your baby is born, you will nurse that baby for about one year or more. When it starts to walk, you will encourage your baby to take steps towards mummy or daddy. You are happy when he or she does. So God also is happy each time you take a step towards Him. Your steps may not be firm yet but He is happy just seeing you take those steps.

183

When the baby starts talking you are happy to see the baby talk; you encourage the baby to talk to you. Even though the words may not make sense to others it's amazing how parents, especially mothers, always understand what their babies are saying. So God wants to hear you yourself speaking to him, even though you may think you are not good enough or don't know what to say. God himself, like the mother, understands the baby. God also understands you. Even when you don't say a word, he is the "God who searches the heart and mind." (Psalm 7: 9) He knows what is in your heart. Talk to him yourself. These are some of the invitations from the scriptures that should encourage you when you come to God.

"Call upon me I will answer you and show you great and mighty things you do not know." (Jeremiah 33: 3)

"Come boldly to the throne of grace that you may receive strength and grace to help you in time of need." (Hebrews 4: 16)

"Come, let us reason together." (Isaiah 1: 18)

All these are personal invitations from God to you. He did not say that you should send Veronica or your pastor or priest or someone else. He says you, yourself should come. Come the way you are; he will meet you at the point at which you are. The first time I knew the Lord the only prayer I said was "Glory to God" in my native language. But because my heart was pure and set on Him, His presence used to hit me so hard that I could not even stand on my feet. I would repeat "Glory to God" over a hundred times a day and that prayer was okay for the Lord because that was all I knew then. Then from there the Holy Spirit moved me on a step at a time. So please come to God yourself; he will meet you at the point of your need and the Holy Spirit will move you on himself at the right time.

Be encouraged

Throughout the Bible we find examples of God answering the prayers of desperate couples who were unable to have children. As my pastor would say: "Each time God opens the womb of a barren woman a miracle child comes out." Sarah and Abraham were barren for a 100 years and then Isaac came along, a child who was to be a blessing to

God's people throughout the earth. Isaac and Rabekah had the same problem and later God blessed them with children. Jacob and Rachel waited for many years to have Joseph, but Joseph later became a prime minister and Deliverer for his people. Ruth the Moabite was barren for ten years but when she gave her life to God, God blessed her with a son named Obed through whom the Christ came into the world. So be encouraged for you also carry seeds of great destiny in you.

My prayer for you

Father, in the name of Jesus Christ, and the authority which you have given me, I stand in unison with my sister reading this book so that you will bless-her and grant her the desires of her heart that her joy may be complete. Father, I thank you that you remain the God of families and you love your people so much. Bring back joy and glory into the home of my sister, that all men will see that you alone are God. I bless you for her life and I thank you that you have done it for her in the name of your son Jesus Christ. Amen. God bless you.

Chapter Twenty

Prayer Points

♦ Stand upon Gods word that you are a joyous mother of children.

♦ Declare the promise of God that whatever you do will prosper and that the Lord will fulfill the number of your days.

♦ Pray against anything that could lead to shock, that could trigger a miscarriage or premature birth or stillbirth.

♦ Pray against the wickedness that destroys in the noonday light.

♦ Curse the root of every demonic entrance of the curse into your family.

♦ Receive a creative miracle by faith where it may be needed in your body.

♦ Reject all manners of diseases like hypertension and diabetes, incompetent cervix and diabetes mellitus.

♦ Pray against anti pregnancy and satanic dreams of blood and activities of pregnancy sucking spirit. *Psalm 58: 2,14-15.*

♦ Pray against weakness during your pregnancy like cramps, varicous veins, pilies and backache and pre-eclampsia.

♦ Pray against any form of blood problems during your pregnancy, declare in Jesus name that you will not need blood transfusion during childbirth.

♦ Pray against evil observers, satanic diary and wicked date calculators.

♦ Declare your healing from any growth or abnormalities of the womb.

♦ Stand against any attempt of the enemy to harm the child in your womb, declare in Jesus' name that you are free from the spirit of fear.

♦ Declare the promise of God that the Lord has satisfied you with long life and good health throughout your pregnancy.

♦ Condemn any tongue that has risen against you and the baby in your womb.

Chapter Twenty One

General Daily Confession

I ascribe to the Lord the glory and strength due to his name. I worship Him in the splendour of his holiness for he has given me his strength and his peace. (Psalm 29:1, 11). I am a blessed and prosperous woman. I am my Father's daughter. I am like a fruitful vine I am a mother of many children. I am fearfully and wonderfully made. My eyes are upon my Father; my face cannot be covered with shame. I am a mother of many children. In Christ I am fruitful. I gaze upon the beauty of the Lord and I seek his face every day. (Psalm 27:4). I have escaped like a bird out of the fowlers' snare; the snare of infertility has been destroyed and I am free. My help is in the name of the Lord, the maker of the heaven and the earth. (Psalm 27:7-8).

I am full of the life of God; congenital disorders are far from me. I am free from any hidden sickness or disease that hides in the body; I am free from the curse of the law. The blessings of Abraham is mine. My children grow well, my vine yields its fruit and my ground produces it's crop and my heavens drops its dew. (Zechariah 8:12).

God himself has made me exceedingly fruitful. (Genesis 17:6). The Lord has made room for me and I am fruitful, I am a fruitful bough, a fruitful bough by a well whose branches ran over the wall. Every day I will rest in the arms of my Father, who has blessed me with the blessing of the heavens above, blessing lying in the deep beneath, blessings of the breast and of the womb. (Genesis 49:22,25).

I flourish like the corn. I blossom like a vine.... I am like a green pine tree; my fruitfulness comes from my Father. (Hosea14: 7-8). Throughout my pregnancy I will bud and blossom and fill the earth with my fruit. For my God has endowed me with His splendour. (Isaiah 27:6, 55:5). I shall not have a miscarriage or any form of abnormal or malformation of the baby in my womb in Jesus' name. I shall be a joyous mother of children, that is God's promise to me and the Word of God is not void of Power so I am confident that the Father Himself has perfected all that which concerns me. (Phillipians 1:6). I thank you Father In Jesus Name.

■ ***Choosing Your Baby's Sex***

Choosing Your Baby's Sex comes as a complement to Veronica Anusionwu's other two titles, "Man, You Are Not Infertile" and "Woman, You Are Not Infertile". In this book the author shares, from the very heart of God, all the information you need to choose the sex of your baby in order to make your joy complete, In this rich and fulfilling book, she also shares her own testimony of how she chose the sex of her own baby.

■ ***Woman, You Are Not Infertile***

The problem of infertility is a serious one, affecting over 100 million couples worldwide, yet at the very heart of God is an overwhelming desire to bless every woman with children. In this book Veronica Anusionwu wants us to turn away from the inadequate areas of medical research to the banquet of rich food prepared for us by Almighty God. All you have to do is say "Yes, God, I want to partake." This is a book written out of love, the kind of love that the Father has for his daughter when he would say, "Woman, you are not infertile, no matter what you have been through or what you have been told, I still want to bless you with children." Designed to assist women who are infertile, this book will also be useful to readers who wish to know more about God.

■ ***Man, You Are Not Infertile***

Until the Lord called her to write this book, Veronica had always thought infertility was only a women's problem, but she discovered that such problems equally affect men (about thirty per cent), while the remaining forty per cent involves both partners. Men, the seed of Adam, hate wasting time on sperm test; they simply want to get on with the command to "multiply and replenish the earth." This book brings good news to those men who have been told they are infertile, and it covers every relevant medical problem which affects male fertility. She then invites us into the banquet of great possbilities prepared by Almighty God for you. Coming from the heart of the Father God, this book tells His beloved sons, "Man You Are Not Infertile."

■ *Blissful Pregnancy, Pain Free Childbirth*

In this book I am going to be sharing with you powerful revelations and Biblical knowledge; how you can have a problem-free pregnancy, having the most wonderful time of your life and bringing forth your baby without long hours of labour pain and painful contractions. This is childbirth the Holy Ghost way. I wish I had enjoyed such revelation knowledge when I had my own children. Register today at the Holy Ghost hospital for a wonderful and blessed nine months of blissful pregnancy and pain free labour.

■ *Oh! God Why All The Miscarriages?*

In this book Veronica examines the issue of miscarriage, premature birth, still birth, incompetent cervix, birth defects from the spiritual perspective. She brings in the medical background before leading us into the Word of God for the solution. She answers questions on miscarriages and still birth, such as: Does God care when you lose a baby? Is it the will of God for mankind to suffer the loss of unborn babies? Is it the will of God for mankind, that a child be born with birth defects? In this book she brings the solution from the Word of God to help you keep that which God has freely given to you.

■ *Who Said You Are Too Old To Conceive?*

In this powerful book Veronica Anusionwu examines the issue of childbirth for an older woman. She bring a medical back ground to what actually happens physically in the body of an older woman; then leads us into the Word of God to supercede the supernatural upon the natural. Veronica declares no woman who wants to have a child should be denied that joy. No matter what her age." She invites the older woman to embark with her on this journey of faith, where you will discover that the Word of God can renew, replace, refreshed, stimulate, rekindle, replenish, rouse, inspire, replace and bring back to vogue and vigour any part of the body. "Yes, you can have that baby if you will dare to believe, that you are not too old to conceive."

SCRUPLES PUBLISHING AND TYPESETTING SERVICES

I know a lot of people are out there that have written or are writing their own book but encounter difficulty in publishing the books. I say this from my own personal experiences. If you are interested in publishing your book and need professional help get in touch with Elizabeth. She will type, edit, proof-read, and typeset your book. She also offers audio transcribing. Whatever your publishing need is. Elizabeth will be able to help you.Contact Elizabeth at - **Scruples** - **PO Box 30303 London NW 10 4WJ - Tel 0208 - 838 - 0007**

THE LORD'S WORD ON HEALING SERIES
Overcoming Infertility Collection
By Veronica Anusionwu
<u>ORDER FORM</u>

Yes, I want:

_____ copy/copies: "Man, You Are Not Infertile" @ £10.00 each

_____ copy/copies: "Woman, You Are Not Infertile" @ £10.99 each

_____ copy/copies: "Choosing Your Baby's Sex" @ £2.95

_____ copy/copies: "Oh God, Why All The Miscarriages?" @ £5.00

_____ copy/copies: "Who Said You Are Too Old To Conceive?" @ £4.99

_____ copy/copies: "Blissful Pregnancy, Pain Free Childbirth" @ £6.00

Please add £1.75 postage and packing per book. Cheques or postal orders should be made payable to - The Lords Word On Healing Publications.

Amount enclosed: _____

Name: _____

Address: _____

_____

_____

PO Box 24604, London E2 9XA

<u>Other Titles In The Lords Word On Healing</u>
<u>Series</u>
By Veronica Anusionwu
<u>ORDER FORM</u>

Yes, I want:

_____ copy/copies: "Triumph Over Impotence"
@ £5.00

_____ copy/copies: "Don't Let that Dying Child Die"
@ £5.00

_____ copy/copies: "This Sickness shall not Return A
2nd Time"@ £4.00 each

_____ copy/copies: "That handicapp Child Can Be
Made Whole"@ £ 6.50

_____ copy/copies: "Triumph Over Cancer"
@ £6.50

Please add £1.75 postage and packing per book. Cheques or postal orders should be made payable to - **The Lords Word On Healing Publications.**

Amount enclosed: _____

Name: _____

Address: _____

_____

Mail to: _____

VERONICA ANUSIONWU, THE LORD'S WORD ON HEALING
MINISTRIES PO BOX 24604, LONDON E2 9XA Tel: 0207-
613-5741

TESTIMONY FORM

The Bible says: *"they overcome him by the blood of the lamb and by the word of their testimony."* Your testimony is important to God and to man. Your testimony glorifies God. Your testimony gives hope to others facing the same situation - to know that if God did it for you He will do it for them. I will be doing a special testimony book in the near future. You can photocopy this form and write your testimony back to us or use a separate sheet of paper. Make sure you send back your testimony to be included in this book. God bless you.

....

....

....

....

....

....

....

....

....

....

....

....

....

....

....

....

....

....

Mail to:

VERONICA ANUSIONWU, THE LORD'S WORD ON HEALING
MINISTRIES PO BOX 24604, LONDON E2 9XA

Please kindly write to me to let me know how this book has helped you, I will be glad to hear from you. Veronica will be running faith clinics in the near future. To find out more about this clinic, please write, enclosing a self-addressed envelope. You can photocopy the faith clinic application form and fill it out and return it to us.

THE LORD'S WORD ON HEALING MINISTRY

<u>FAITH CLINIC APPLICATION FORM</u>

The purpose of the faith clinic is to help those who may need someone to stand with them in prayer and faith to receive all they need from God. The faith clinic is designed to help build faith in God and Jesus Christ for those who need it.

Answer these questions truthfully. This will help us to determine what faith class you will need to attend.

DATE: _____

NAME: _____

AGE: _____

ADDRESS: _____

_____

1) How long have you been trying for a baby?

_____

2) Have you undergone any medical check-up to di-

agnose the cause of infertility?

3)   What was the diagnosis?

_____

_____

_____

4)   Will you be willing to participate in a series of faith teachings from the Bible to build your faith to overcome your limitations?   **Tick Box**

YES ☐   **NO** ☐

5)   If you have been trying to conceive but have not gone through any medical check up.

YES ☐   **NO** ☐

6)   Do you have any children?

YES ☐   **NO** ☐

7)   Have you suffered any miscarriage?

YES ☐   **NO** ☐

8)   Have you lost any child at birth?

9)   **YES** ☐   **NO** ☐

Is there anything you want to tell us that will help in deciding what faith clinic you need to attend.? (Write on a separate sheet of paper if necessary.)

YES ☐   **NO** ☐

Mail to:

Veronica Anusionwu, The Lords Word On Healing Ministries PO BOX 24604, London E2 9XA.

Tel:0207-613-5741

Covenant Partners Form

Dear, partner,

God has called me to bring the Healing Gospel of Jesus to the world. To accomplish this vision I am going to need Faith Covenant Partners. I have prayed that the Lord will send me faithful men and women who will stand with me both financially and spiritually to fulfil this vision. If God is laying it on your heart to partnership with me please respond now.

As a covenant partner I and my prayer team will pray for you every day, will stand with you in faith whenever you need us.

In return I will expect you to sow seed monthly into this ministry or as the spirit of God leads you. Pray for me and my staff as the Spirit of God leads you.

When you sow into the work of God the Bible promises you these benefits: **Protection** (Mal:3 10-11) . **Favour** (Luke 6:38). **Fianacial prosperity** (Deut :8 18).

Please complete this response form and return it to me today.
If you have a prayer request please send it on a seperate sheet of paper.

Name: _____ _____

Address: _____

_____

_____

Tel _____

Mail to:
Veronica Anusionwu, The Lords Word On Healing Ministries
PO BOX 24604, London E2 9XA.
Tel:0207-613-5741